AVOIDING
DISASTER

HOW TO KEEP YOUR BUSINESS GOING WHEN CATASTROPHE STRIKES

JOHN LAYE

JOHN WILEY & SONS, INC.

For general information on our other products and services please contact our Customer Care Department within the U.S. at (800) 762-2974, outside the United States at (317) 572-3993 or fax (317) 572-4002.

Wiley also publishes its books in a variety of electronic formats. Some content that appears in print may not be available in electronic books.

ISBN 0-471-22915-6

Printed in the United States of America

10 9 8 7 6 5 4 3 2 1

Contents

Foreword

John Laye has produced a well-written book on a subject of intense current interest—how to avoid disasters and how to keep your business going even if a disaster occurs. It is applicable worldwide—to natural disasters such as earthquakes and windstorms, to terrorist action and to other disasters caused by people, their activities, and their technologies.

The recent events in New York and Washington, D.C., have shown us that terrorism can strike practically anywhere and can take many forms. Perhaps that was a surprise to many of us. It should not have been. It was little surprise to those few New Yorkers who were concerned enough to prepare their people and businesses. It was an even smaller surprise in Europe, where companies have been affected by terrorism for decades and many companies have taken actions to reduce the potential impacts.

Throughout the United States, we are vulnerable to natural disasters, no matter where we live or conduct business. The Northeast coast and the entire North of the country is subject to severe winter storms. The rest of the East Coast and the Gulf Coast are subject to hurricanes. All of the West coast is subject to very large earthquakes. Those areas account for about two thirds of the population and business activity of the country. In addition, the rest of the country is subject to tornados, flooding, and draught, and some regions, such as the Mississippi River Valley, are exposed to infrequent but very large earthquakes.

Events that lead to disasters are inevitable. But with proper foresight and management, the resulting losses can be greatly reduced; sometimes they can be nearly eliminated. For example, we do not have the technology to prevent earthquakes (we do not even have the technology to predict them yet), but we have the technology to prevent the damage that earthquakes cause. That is the case with all hazards — we possess the management skills and the technologies to reduce their effects dramatically.

An excellent example is the Anheuser Busch Company. Their brewery in the San Fernando Valley of Southern California sat astride the epicenter of the 1994 Northridge earthquake, the costliest in U.S. history. Barely three months before the earthquake, management in Van Nuys and in the distant headquarters in St. Louis had completed a strengthening program to reduce potential earthquake damage in that facility. Anheuser Busch spent about $10 million strengthening buildings and equipment and training its people, which saved the company more than $1 billion in direct damage and business interruptions, and probably a number of lives. In the midst of a disaster area, the company was able to resume business in four days. Some of their neighboring companies went bankrupt because of the earthquake. After the event, no one questioned the need for the expenditures, but it took considerable foresight and business acumen to procure the funds and to complete the work in light of all other demands on expenditures and time.

The main reason that disasters occur today is the widespread lack of the necessary management skills to bring forth the organization and the technologies that avoid disasters. John Laye describes vividly this problem and then systematically lays out the solution, which involves upper as well as middle management while organizing and training. Few people are as well equipped as John Laye to address these issues because disaster management is relatively new and only a few people have his extensive background. Fewer still bridge the gap among field response, research, planning, and management. John Laye has been part of the evolution of disaster management from its nearly exclusive emphasis on response to the current emphasis on scenario-based mitigation, planning, recovery, and training. He is also a fervent advocate of the emerging, but not yet widely implemented, advanced management concept of close government-corporate coordination.

This book presents what is needed to establish and maintain a successful business continuity program. It addresses how to survive disasters and how to avoid them by containing an event—preventing it from becoming a crisis, then evolving into a disaster, or worse. Formal training opportunities are too few to accommodate the many managers who need this information. John Laye has provided it admirably.

Peter Yanev
Orinda, California

Introduction

I wrote this book for several categories of managers—the professionals I listen to and trade information with all over the world. First are managers who got the task of developing plans as a collateral duty, in addition to the position description for which they were hired. Often, that additional task was given as though it were a relatively simple project that any competent manager could finish easily in a short time without much effort. True enough, it can be approached as a series of very manageable tasks, but many highly competent managers will confirm that successfully fitting those tasks together is anything but simple. In addition, the notion that an effective business continuity plan is going to be finished quickly is the stuff of urban legends.

The chapters in this volume were put together in a series that lays out the many tasks and couples them together in a practical sequence—which might not match a lecture hall's theoretical approach but was designed to work in a manager's real world.

The second group this book should help is the senior executives who initiate and direct a business continuity program and select its managers. Although the whole book should be helpful, I know the demands on their time will limit absorbing all of it, so Chapter 4 is expressly for them. In fact, the original subtitle, "How to Keep Your Market Share

When It Hits the Fan," was created to get senior executives' notice. I wrote it as if I had 20 minutes to tell them in conversation how to judge the managers' qualifications, what guidance to give their organizations, how to track the program as it develops, and what is reasonable to expect. It also occurred to me that a subordinate with business continuity responsibilities might want to put the book in a senior executive's in box, with Chapter 4 bookmarked (it's not too late for that).

Another group I was thinking of as this book unfolded is the managers who have admirably taken their time, toil, and treasure (a useful phrase that is repeated elsewhere in this book) to educate themselves about what began as *emergency management,* evolved through *disaster recovery* into *business continuity* and *crisis management,* and will likely be driven by comparative costs into *disaster avoidance.* Because memory fades with time and because the profession has continued to evolve, this book is designed to provide an affordable updated desk reference.

While writing, I tried to keep the book on track by thinking of what I wish someone with a lot of experience had laid out for me when I began planning, training, and testing over 20 years ago. Of course, the business continuity profession did not exist as such when a few of us started adapting our experience, our mentors' advice, and researchers' data into what has evolved into today's more structured laws, regulations, standards, and guidelines, so our mentors could not lay out a logically structured path for programs. I've tried to do that in this book.

Not that everything is now engraved in stone and unchanging—I am happy to say that the body of professional knowledge continues to grow with experience and research, so the final chapter was put into the book to help managers track ongoing developments. My wish is that readers will find that this book has most of what is needed to establish and maintain a successful business continuity program, which will in turn let your organization avert that disaster that can take it down.

My final wish is that readers will communicate with me about any omissions, lack of clarity, or differences of opinion that this book calls to mind, as well as new developments. I value readers' ideas as colleagues and am convinced that discussions can contribute positively to the ongoing evolution of our profession.

This book is affectionately dedicated to Jeanne, Linda, Russ, and to my several colleagues who, on hearing for the umpteenth time my complaint that there were no good, comprehensive texts, told me to stop whining and start writing.

Chapter 1

Getting Started

Answering the Whys

When I said my business was preventing disasters, a woman from Hong Kong asked me, "How can you stop a typhoon?" Of course, I can't, and neither can anyone else on the planet, but we *can* avoid disasters. I wrote this book to share what I have learned about not just how to survive disasters, but how to *avoid* them.

When we give it a little thought, the word "disaster" really refers to a disruptive event that has severe impacts on us humans and our creations. That includes our ongoing business or services.[1] A typhoon, known outside the Far East as a hurricane or cyclone, is just one example of a disruptive event that need not be a disaster for *your* organization, even if it passes right over you. Nor does any other damaging event have to be a disaster, whether caused by humans, technology, or the forces of nature. This leads to three whys.

Why Number 1: Why would anyone be so bold as to say that your organization — and that includes business, government, and nonprofit organizations — can truly avoid disasters? Because we can. That's the short answer. And in this book there are case histories to prove it. Please keep reading.

Why Number 2: You might concede that we *can*, but why

spend time, toil, and treasure preparing to mitigate the out-comes of events that won't be that expensive? To put it an-other way, where is the return on investment? Of course, expensive mitigation for an event with small impacts makes no sense. But that's not what we'll be talking about in this book. It is important to know the difference between an event with small potential impacts and one that can bring down the organization, and then apply common sense to get cost effective preparations. It doesn't cost that much to learn which are the really dangerous events for your organization: events that can spiral out of control, expanding from a crisis to become a disaster, then inflating into a catastrophe—something that can put your organization's survival in ques-tion.

Why Number 3: Given today's pace of business, including government's business of providing services, and the ex-pectations of your organization's customers (whether your organization calls them customers, clients, taxpayers, con-stituents, or whatever doesn't matter), no manager or policy maker can afford to be regarded as so inept that he or she lacks the foresight to make effective preparations, minimiz-ing the impacts of dangerous events.

Government managers reading this might be tempted to think that no circumstances could become so severe as to threaten their situation, but that is a dangerous assumption. For one example, in the Loma Prieta earthquake (which the popular media often called the San Francisco earthquake) of 1989, the City of San Francisco's response and recovery efforts were widely perceived as mismanaged. That per-ception became a major factor in bringing down San Francisco's incumbent mayor,[2] whose successor naturally appointed a lot of new department heads. The annals of gov-ernment are replete with similar accounts.

For example, Seattle's World Trade Organization (WTO)

riots caused not only retail business losses because a great many people avoided the Christmas shopping season in downtown Seattle; there were severe governmental and political impacts as well. As an illustration, in the next election, for the first time in 65 years, an incumbent Seattle mayor was defeated in a primary election.[3] When asked if the WTO rioting contributed to Mayor Paul Schell's defeat, University of Washington political science professor David Olson replied that it had and that "we can make educated conjectures that voters did sense less than adequate preparation for and response to the WTO protest, [and] it went beyond WTO."[4] In other words, the government's customers became sensitized to the management of other events. California's power crisis is associated with lowered approval ratings for Governor Gray Davis, whose presidential aspirations were widely discussed — and there are many more instances of governmental impacts because of inadequate preparations that made foreseeable events politically dangerous. It isn't just businesses whose survival is at risk.

Speaking of businesses, let's briefly recall some case histories of events that either did or did not expand into disasters and then further inflate to become catastrophes. We shall see that the survival of even major transnational corporations can be threatened.

Bhopal, India, was the site of a Union Carbide plant that made insecticide and fertilizer. If ever a plant were constructed for a worthy cause — making a product to help feed masses of people — Bhopal was that plant. An intermediate stage in the process involved liquid methyl isocyanate, which expands massively and becomes a poisonous gas when combined with water. Sadly, tragically, that's what happened. The gas escaped during the night, and thousands living around the Union Carbide plant died. Many more were severely injured or even disabled for life. Instead of reaping the benefit intended by Union Carbide for so many people, thousands became invalids for India's struggling economy to support through the government. Of course, the event was seen as poorly managed. The almost inevitable investigations brought other perceptions of inadequate management into focus, much as occurred in Seattle. The results were also predictable.

Bhopal marked the beginning of Union Carbide's downsizing from a multienterprise, corporate Goliath to a much smaller corporation concentrated on its traditional competencies. In rapid sequence, Carbide (1) had difficulty renewing liability insurance; (2) reached a severance agreement with its former chairman; (3) faced a hostile takeover bid by GAF Corporation, expending large amounts of time, toil, and treasure (it recapitalized to defend itself); (4) sold its worldwide battery operations;[5] (5) sold Home & Automotive Products;[6] (6) sold its worldwide Agricultural Products business;[7] and (7) dissolved the corporation, restructuring as UCC Holdings and other companies.[8]

Readers from not-for-profit charitable organizations could be thinking that disruptive events are unlikely to trigger major impacts in their organizations, so let us go back to the Loma Prieta earthquake and examine another case.

People and organizations had contributed money that they thought would be applied to San Francisco Bay Area earthquake relief, but they discovered that a significant part of their gifts had been sent elsewhere. There was a lot of dismay, which was reflected in media stories. Perhaps the greater damage during and beyond that period was the loss of trust and confidence over time.

The adverse reactions were sufficient that $60 million had to be returned to the Bay Area, and the Northern California Disaster Preparedness Network was formed to see that the money was spent on earthquake-related local issues.

By now, the point should be clear. No matter which sector an organization occupies, failing to prepare to manage disruptive events and allowing them to progress from event through disaster to catastrophe can have major impacts—even putting the organization's survival at risk. One of the most worrying aspects for conscientious managers is how much enduring damage can be done to the confidence that people must have in their organizations to ensure their futures. We shall see in future chapters that several impact categories need to be assessed to discover how much and what kinds of preparations are needed. Time and again, the lesson comes through: it is necessary to plan to manage events before they start that graveyard spiral[9] down into disasters and on to catastrophes.

Of course, there are a lot of useful details in case histories of familiar events, so read on as I review several incidents to hear some that had good outcomes, including an exception where near breakeven was achieved through solid guiding principles, even with no formal plan in place.

Let us begin by distinguishing among disruptive events, disasters, and worse. Regarding *disruptive events,* humans have experienced a long list, and it is included in this book.[10] Corporate business continuity professionals usually call it a *threat list,* but terminology is not yet uniform in this rapidly growing profession. Government professionals use the term *hazards list,* but there are few differences between business managers' threat lists and government emergency managers' hazards lists.

Broadly speaking, threats divide into three categories: natural disasters, human-caused events, and technological accidents. In some lists, the header "human-caused" is replaced by "anthropogenic," which means the same thing but makes people reach for their dictionaries, which in turn makes some lecturers feel important. The fact that a tech-

nological accident such as a power outage involves something crafted by humans and can therefore be thought of as
human-caused—if we humans had put it together properly,
there wouldn't have been an accident, right?—is a quibble.
Besides, because human-*caused* events and events that start
themselves in human-*made* systems usually have different
characteristics and call for different preventive or mitigating actions, the threats listed in Appendix A of Chapter 2
uses those three categories. As we shall see, just how a disruptive event starts is usually not very important until after
the principal management has taken steps to stop escalation
toward disaster.

■ CASE ONE: A DISRUPTIVE EVENT THAT DID NOT BECOME A DISASTER

The first to be hit in the anthrax-by-mail attacks on American organizations was the *National Enquirer*'s publisher,
Florida-based American Media. Sadly, a company employee
became the first anthrax fatality, and health authorities
quickly quarantined the building. Faced with both a closed
facility and commitments to deadlines (the *National Enquirer* alone has a circulation greater than 2.7 million[11]), the
company implemented its hurricane plan, in which employees work from their homes, and publication continued.[12]

■ CASE TWO: WITH A DISASTER UPON IT, THE ORGANIZATION BOUNCED BACK

After the catastrophe of September 11, 2001, there were
many public pronouncements to the effect that the day's attacks had been a complete surprise, marking the first warning that terrorism's evils were abroad and had become

something that could cross boundaries and enter the lives of ordinary citizens. Further, the pronouncements noted that this was an evil that was *calculated* for its impacts against ordinary people.

But it wasn't the first warning. The first warning came in 1982—almost exactly ten years earlier.

On September 29, 1982, three people in Chicago's suburbs died because cyanide had been introduced into Extra Strength Tylenol as it sat on retail shelves before the customers purchased and took it. Retrospectively, the event had all the characteristics of a well-planned terrorist attack. It struck at innocents. It was calculated for maximum media impact. It used a vehicle unlikely to arouse suspicion. The evil's instigator was separated by time and distance before people were confronted by the impacts. Ultimately, five people were dead from the cyanide, which transformed a productive humanitarian agent into "an agent for doing evil to its unsuspecting consumers."[13]

McNeil Laboratories made and distributed Tylenol, and Johnson & Johnson was McNeil's parent company. Working in teamwork, both companies' executives quickly formed a set of priority goals based on the credo laid down more than 50 years ago by Robert Wood Johnson, the son of Johnson & Johnson's founder. As Steven Fink[14] noted, the credo specifies that the company has four responsibilities: to the consumers, to the employees, to the communities that they serve, and to the stockholders—in that order. With the credo before them, the policy-level executives set the goals for managing the disaster. Their goals, in order, were to stop the attacks, to determine the cause of the attacks, and to help those injured by the attacks. The policy directives of both the credo and the executives' plan are clear, unequivocal, and directed for maximum beneficial effect. We shall see that these elements are necessary for success when organizations are faced with a disaster. In this case, the directives led the companies to ask retailers to remove every container of the product from their shelves everywhere in the United States. Just before the decision to sweep the shelves, Tylenol had 35 percent of the billion-dollar analgesic market.[15] Immediately after, its market share was zero. However, within four years, Tylenol was back with 98 percent of the sales figures it had enjoyed before that decision.[16]

The many steps taken and the reasoning used by McNeil and Johnson & Johnson in the four years between September 1982 and 1986 have become management course cases cited as examples of lucid decision making under stress,[17] but the point here is that quick, decisive, and well-reasoned management in the face of a disaster in progress saved the brand.

■ CASE THREE: A DISRUPTIVE EVENT WITH TWO VASTLY DIFFERENT OUTCOMES

On March 17, 2000, the Philips Electronics microchip manufacturing plant in Albuquerque, New Mexico, experienced a lightning strike that started a fire. The fire was quickly extinguished, but the damage was enough to take down the chip-making line, and there was little prospect for restoring production of this critical part, which was in short supply. The plant made chips for cellular[18] telephones and had two principal customers, Ericsson and Nokia. Nokia noted the decline in chip deliveries from Philips and quickly contacted senior management, who began close coordination with Philips. Nokia was able to continue telephone deliveries to distributors, who delivered to retailers, and so on to consumers, while Ericsson discovered what had happened—too late.[19] With a shift in market share, Ericsson's situation has by now been well documented in the business press.

Having illustrated the three "whys" that usually occur to managers, answered them, and provided several case histories to demonstrate that preparations pay, let us now turn our attentions to the rudiments of how to become prepared. Let's call it Basic Stuff.

Chapter 2

Basic Stuff

The core of this chapter is devoted to recognizing and applying 5 of the 10 principles that professionals accept as essential to prepare for and to keep disruptive events from blowing up into *emergencies,* which can then grow into *disasters* and go on to become *catastrophes* that sink the organization. This chapter also addresses people issues that are the basis for further planning. It adds the following mundane items: an Emergency Response Team (ERT) training syllabus and information on how to select team members, a good supplies and equipment list for the response team, and a layout that lets a conference room become a crisis management center. Supplies, equipment, and connections crisis management groups need are listed. How to select the right managers to become team members and how to assign functions among the team's members are also discussed. All those follow the 10 principles for developing a good defense before the inevitable happens, and your organization is hit.

Let us begin with something even more basic than those 10 principles. Disaster avoidance occurs at three levels, or categories of activities, in virtually all organizations. At the top is the *policy* level, or *senior management.* Where the customers are served, the widgets are made, or value is otherwise added (the profit centers), *operations* occur. Sandwiched between them is *management* (hence the term, *middle management*). When thinking of the 10 principles, think also of the level where those principles should be applied.

A recent happy development is agreement among the principal certifying professional groups about the 10 principles that form the bases for developing programs that can effectively and efficiently manage preparations before, responses during, and restorations after such events. As a foundation for that, these groups came to recognize that they had constituencies in many nations around the world. The profession has become truly international.

Who are these professional groups? Probably the premier organization certifying members is the Business Continuity Institute[1] (BCI), headquartered in Worcester, England. In the United States, the Disaster Recovery Institute International[2] (DRII) has probably issued the largest number of certificates to corporate managers. It is headquartered in Falls Church, Virginia. The International Association of Emergency Managers[3] (IAEM), also headquartered in Falls Church, most likely has issued more certificates to local government emergency managers than have other certifiers. There are many other groups for professionals (most regionally based), but these are the principal certifiers. Two other organizations should be mentioned for recognizing the principles: the U.S. Department of Labor established the content and process for developing industrial and other corporate emergency management plans in the U.S. Code of Federal Regulations,[4] and the National Fire Protection Association in recent years developed a Standard that is essentially a match.[5]

And what are these 10 principles or steps that define the process that so greatly reduces the risks for both corporate and government organizations? Let us use the BCI's words and sequence to describe them.

■ STEP 1: PROJECT INITIATION

Probably the most difficult part of any project is getting started, and projects to avoid disasters are no exception. It begins with establishing a goal, which makes it a little dangerous — dangerous because once they begin, people want to continue down the path, and it is therefore essential to make the best practical effort at defining a goal. It is possible to change the goal if it becomes apparent that the original was not the best, but it is difficult. Another potential problem is that a disaster-avoidance goal is a strategic decision, and thinking strategically is not a habit for most managers in today's world. It requires both a long-term viewpoint and a broad perspective, encompassing the whole organization and its operating environment. Based on experience, I recommend setting your goal broad enough that the inevitable snipers cannot claim that the project is not making progress, as well as making sure that it defines improvement. One thing I will not do is say that there is a magic phrase guaranteed to meet all needs. Realistically, every organization has its own culture; words get used differently from organization to organization, so choose what is most likely to be accepted within yours.

The essence of the goal, however, can be simply stated. It should contain three elements. One element should refer to your organization's mission statement (the *real* mission, not a statement designed for public relations purposes or crafted to win a morale-building contest) and commit the project to supporting the mission. Another element is recognition of serious risk to the organization's future. This may require some educational effort at the highest levels. For success, every project needs a champion there. Another element establishes that it will greatly benefit the organization and its people, who are the backbone, bonds, and doers.

You may discover one or more senior managers who are already motivated (perhaps they have had real experience with disasters that were not avoided, or barely avoided), and you may be able to put convincing evidence before others (video news clips and interviews with other senior managers are good, but direct conversations with senior managers who have dodged the bullet are better still). Frankly, that's what Chapter 1 was designed to help readers with. No matter how convinced you may be that a disaster-avoidance project is essential, do not risk your professional reputation (not to mention sanity) on internal guerilla warfare in the form of an unsponsored project. If the project lacks one or more champions, there will be no budget. No budget, no resources. No resources, no support by colleagues. All those are hard enough to come by because at least a few other managers will see any new project as competition to their own requirements. Find at least one champion and keep sending positive feedback.

Objectives will be needed shortly after words defining the project's goal are chosen. They should be subordinated to the project's goal; they should be independent; they should be memorable; they should be measurable; and, above all, they should be doable. There should not be a lot of them. A number around five works best.

Their independence is important because unforeseen opportunities can shift priorities. For practical purposes, this means that a project may be put on hold or slowed down as resources or key managers' time is diverted. To support the organization as a whole ("be a team player"), disaster-avoidance projects should maintain flexibility by having objectives that can be achieved one at a time and then resumed when resources loosen up. Recall the necessity for strategic thinking cited earlier. This is an example.

When one or more high-level champions have been found, some accepted practices advocate developing the project plan and budget. In my experience, the next two steps—risk assessment and business impact estimating[6]—are essential to provide reasonable parameters for budgeting and defining the other resources essential to do more than outline a plan. A good case can be made that we need to go beyond those two steps to the next one, developing business continuity strategies, but I will not try to take the discussion that far. This is, after all, a book for practical managers (both program managers and their bosses[7]) who want to get started toward avoiding disasters. For practical purposes, at this point it is too early to do detailed budgeting and program planning. Wait until you have the risk assessment and business impact estimates in hand.

Which brings us to risk assessment as the second step.

■ STEP 2: RISK ASSESSMENT

A risk assessment is produced in three stages. The initial stage is threat evaluation. One must determine, *for a specific location,* which threats are present. For natural hazards, historic data is usually available from the local government's Office of Emergency Services. Here again, terminology varies. In parts of the United States, that function often resides in an organization called Civil Defense. In other countries it has other names; Russia, for example, calls theirs the Ministry of Major Emergencies. At the national level in the United States, it's the Federal Emergency Management Agency (FEMA). Where local emergency management does not have a ready list of natural hazards, the Natural Hazards Center at the University of Colorado[8] is an excellent resource.

As described earlier, there are also threats from human-caused (or anthropogenic) and accidental (technological) events. For a reasonably complete listing of threats, see Appendix A of this chapter.

After the threats for a specific location have been identified, two other factors are needed to assess them. To answer "How much should we fear the threats that are present?" two factors are magnitude and frequency[9] — in everyday English, "How big can one of these get?" and "How often does one of these happen?" The purpose of gathering these data is to create brief stories or scenarios about two or three of the threats that can have very severe effects.

The second stage of risk assessment then becomes creating the scenarios. Two or three are all that's needed because they will be presented to your organization's business unit managers, who will not have time to read and understand more than two or three. That means that great precision in developing all there is to know about every threat for a given site is unnecessary. Take the effects of two or three of the most severe threats and make a one- or two-paragraph scenario that a business unit manager will have time to read and quickly comprehend. For example:

At ten in the morning of a normal working day, a large earthquake strikes our region. The shaking continues for well over a minute, causing furniture to move about the rooms and wall hangings, ceiling tiles, and shelves' contents to fall. The connections to machines break, and heavy machines that are not secured to structural members break loose. Many fall over. The air fills with dust, and the lights fail. Moving objects and falling debris cause injuries. Employees help each other evacuate after the shaking, and most reach their designated outside relocation points and are accounted for. A walk-around survey outside reveals that parts of the building are likely to collapse. The building is judged to be too dangerous to enter, even to get vital records.

■ STEP 3: BUSINESS IMPACT ANALYSIS

The business unit managers' introduction to the principal risks begins the business impact analysis, which is stage three of a risk assessment.

What is needed back from the business unit managers are answers to fundamental questions centered on "What effect will this scenario have on your unit's ability to function?" Managers should respond by outlining what production or services will be interrupted by the different scenarios that you gave them. They should also consider the requirements to resume operations. To prompt this, a questionnaire will be helpful. Items to be addressed are employee requirements, vital records, telecommunications, information systems support, logistics (which can be pretty elaborate for manufacturing and processing operations), outsourced services, and other things that are specific to any organization that intends to avoid disasters.

From the responses, identify critical functions (essential to the continued stability of the organization), including interdependencies, and begin to discover probable priorities for recovery. Why priorities? Inevitably, when a large or prolonged threat becomes reality, organizations discover that they must deal with too many problems being pursued by too few resources. Probably the best the program can produce at this point is provisional recovery time objectives for each of the business functions whose managers provided feedback. You have no doubt noted that this paragraph is full of conditional words: "begin to," "probable," and "provisional." This is because corporations are usually unwilling to let very many people know exactly which business units contribute what percentage of gross receipts, and even less so what their contributions are to net profits. On top of such deliberate obscuration, very few organizations want people outside or inside to know what their vulnerabilities are. So the program manager at this point is (quite necessarily) piercing a veil, and there will be some resistance. Not to worry—get what you can for now. More will unfold as the business unit managers learn or are told to trust you, and Chapter 11 has some recommendations to help develop the needed information.

To help make a case for a disaster avoidance program with impacts that senior managers can appreciate beyond the dollar amounts that business unit managers can furnish, you can incorporate additional types. They are listed as Appendix A of Chapter 4 and are placed there to make it easy for senior managers to evaluate program presentations.

What have we so far? Of the 10 steps to a business continuity plan, we have (1) initiated the program, (2) assessed the threats, and (3) converted threat data into scenarios to obtain basic business impact estimates. The fourth step is to develop business continuity strategies. Note the plural— strategies.

■ STEP 4: BUSINESS CONTINUITY STRATEGIES

There are three general strategies: continuous operation, rapid restoration, and recovery. As a practical matter, the organization's very short-term business cycle defines these strategies. The concern is how a given strategy *appears* to outside clients and others. For example, a bank's currency traders operate all 24 hours of each day. Continuous operation in that office means that being unable to trade for one minute may be unacceptable. To meet a zero downtime reliability requirement is very expensive in both cost and preparation efforts. At the same bank, its trust department may be open from nine in the morning until five in the afternoon, and never on a weekend or a holiday. Acceptable recovery time for that group is usually measured in hours of a working day. The same bank has administrative functions (purchasing, personnel, etc.), and for that group recovery within a few days may be acceptable.

Undoubtedly you have noticed my continued use of conditional words and phrases such as "usually" and "may be acceptable." It is not practical on these pages to determine which strategies belong to which business functions. Let me just caution planners that your organization's senior managers must make informed decisions about which strategies to use for which business *function*—and when. The italics are meant to acknowledge a complicating factor. A given business unit is likely to have more than one function. Some functions require one strategy; some can use another. The "—and when" acknowledges a second factor, for which a simple example provides a good illustration.

For most corporations, reputation is critically important. One way reputations are evaluated is by how promptly the corporation pays its obligations. For that reason, the loss of the business function that issues paychecks on the day after payday can usually be overcome with a relatively leisurely recovery strategy. In the same organization the loss of check-cutting capability just before payroll is to be calculated and paid calls for a very different strategy. You will undoubtedly recognize similar situations in your organization's operations. When the impact estimates are discussed with business unit managers, be alert to those situations. They will form the basis for recommended strategies to senior management.[10] At that point rudimentary costs-benefits tradeoffs should be presented.

After proposing strategies for at least those business functions critical[11] to the organization's mission (please recall that this chapter started by asserting that the goal statement should contain an element referring to your organization's mission), the next step (fifth of 10) is setting up an internal mechanism for emergency responses and managing emergency operations. The rest of this chapter will discuss the response phase—the period during and immediately after a physically damaging event—and what must be done to stop and control damage. This includes damage to people, systems, and physical property. Another "Why?" is a likely thought here, and three answers come up immediately.

■ STEP 5: EMERGENCY RESPONSE

First, as pointed out in Chapter 1, emergencies not quickly dealt with are likely to escalate. Firefighters often say "All fires start small," and that's a good expression of a basic principle. If your organization has in-house ERTs, it can rapidly and definitively deal with a number of events ranging from necessary first aid through releases of hazardous materials (hazmats). Second, when a major emergency taxes the community's resources, overwhelming the usually prompt and efficient firefighters, utility crews, and emergency medical services, why be helpless? Third, the presence of the organization's own ERTs will not go unnoticed by the employees. They will quickly realize that the in-house ERTs will be at the scene of any emergency well before outside responders can arrive. Their ability to stabilize situations and often to reverse deteriorating ones is a great way to help employees realize that the organization has their interests in mind. Thus, it becomes an employee morale and retention asset.

Fortunately, the threat evaluation process described earlier in this chapter identified what events are probable, how often, and how severe they can be, along with their effects. The process also put those data into brief stories—the scenarios. These can help define what ERTs need to know and what supplies and equipment they will need to match their knowledge. Later in this chapter, recruiting, training, and equipping ERTs will be discussed. Just now, the second part of this fifth step is important.

The first part established ERTs. In a major event, particularly when a natural hazard materializes, these ERTs will often have to operate alone because the scale of the event will engage all available outside response resources (i.e., fire and rescue, police, emergency medical, and utilities). Even where there is a wealth of outside emergency responders and a well-developed mutual aid system, getting distant resources or reserves to the many emergency scenes is going to take longer than most organizations will want to wait. In addition, when the immediate emergency (i.e., danger to lives and property) has been subdued, the outside emergency responders must return to a ready status, leaving corporations to deal with damage control, cleanup, and restoration of their own infrastructures. In any of those situations, a management function is needed. So the complement to ERTs is emergency management, which also requires a team approach.

Volumes have been written about emergency management. I have been involved in the training of emergency management teams since before FEMA's course development began in 1982.[12] Thousands of managers from a great many governmental agencies and communities in the United States and other countries have now received integrated emergency management training, and thousands more have received similar training through courses in the private sector. Although there are numerous adaptations for varying local needs and for varying corporate cultures, there are common functions. Readers should realize that a complete treatment of managing ERTs would require at least one additional book, so this book will discuss only the basic framework and what I believe are fundamental requirements, plus a few of the most important lessons learned over the past quarter century. There is one very important thing to learn and remember about emergency management teams:

> However carefully an organization goes through the steps, and however well drawn its emergency plans are, it is the emergency management team's proficiency that will achieve success and efficiency and ultimately determine the organization's reputation when a threat materializes and becomes a major event.

There is an irrational but often-expressed hope that someone will rise to the occasion in every emergency. More often, people fall back on their level of training.[13] Thus, the importance of a well-trained and frequently rehearsed team is difficult to overemphasize.

What are the common elements among virtually all emergency management teams?

1. A group selected to bring knowledge and expertise together to deal with major events that threaten the ability of the organization to perform its mission.

2. The ability to gather quickly information about what is happening.

3. The ability to share that information efficiently among the team's members.

4. The ability to

    a. decide on an immediate course of action for a given problem, or

    b. send the information necessary to senior management for a decision on that problem.

5. The ability to identify and direct resources to carry out those decisions.

6. The ability to monitor how effectively those decisions are being carried out, adjusting direction as necessary.

There are numerous adjunct functions that Emergency Management Teams should perform (and most do), but these are the essentials to keep an event from entering that graveyard spiral and descending from event to crisis to disaster to catastrophe, *provided the team's proficiency is maintained*. The next thing to think about is what form the team's organization should assume. In other words, what framework best defines the lines of authority and communication for the team?

The good news is that several models exist. The better news is that where the model matches the organization's culture, it will probably be effective, and the more the team practices and adjusts it, the more efficiently it will work. If you will take that statement as your point of departure, I will outline a couple of models currently in favor.

First is the classic military command staff structure, referred to by many emergency response agencies as the Incident Command System (ICS). Its basic form looks like Figure 2.1. Government managers in California will recognize this model as the organizational form required by the Governor's Office of Emergency Services and called the Standardized Emergency Management System (SEMS) in that state. Above the manager, of course, is the organization's senior management.

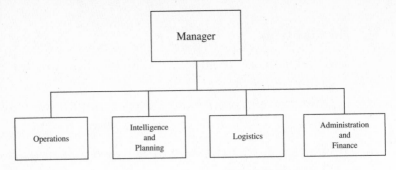

Figure 2.1 The Incident Command System's Basic Form

A connection to senior management is required not only for sending some issues there for decisions, but also for permitting senior management to monitor what is going on in the emergency management team and to intervene when necessary—but *only* when necessary. Below the lower line of boxes are the operational forces and resources that the emergency management team directs to keep emergencies or crises from escalating. The manager's principal duty is to ensure *integrated emergency management,* meaning that incoming and specialized information is shared (to reduce the probability of unintended consequences—another way to say "bad decisions"), that decisions directing actions are derived jointly, and that ordered actions are coordinated.

Another model[14] uses existing departments[15] within the company. As with the ICS, there is a central authority figure whose duties include liaison with senior management and ensuring that integrated emergency management is practiced. In this model "central" can be a good choice of term. There may be no resemblance to the traditional hierarchical organization chart. Indeed, my recent experience with small- to medium-sized family companies and some very large high-tech firms has been that formal organizational models do not exist in a number of cases. Where that is the case, following the company's existing practice removes at least one cause of discomfort during major emergencies. The

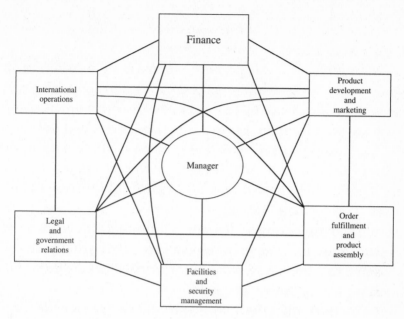

Figure 2.2 Practices' Connections for Managing Emergencies

model in Figure 2.2 provides a generic example of organization for managing emergencies inside such companies.

You will notice that the lines have been drawn to show that direct liaison is encouraged between every organizational group represented on an emergency management team. In fact, they were drawn to represent graphically the concept of integrated emergency management. Please go back and look at the previous ICS diagram (Figure 2.1) in the same light. Direct liaison among each one of the five boxes depicted there is equally important.

Of course, other models exist, as was previously stated. The two models just depicted have great advantages. The ICS has simplicity. In addition, it mimics what has become the most-used system for managing field operations during emergencies. The second is a *generic* model to illustrate using a company's in-place organization. Although it may look difficult for an outsider to use, the company's managers are accustomed to it, so one like theirs should contribute to their comfort level in stressful situations.

No matter how many times one has done it, whether in simulations or in reality, managing a major emergency is stressful, which leads to people issues. Not everyone is going to be an effective manager during crises. Some will not fully recover after dealing with such events. There are some things that can be done to minimize the effects that major emergencies will have on people. Again, volumes have been written about the relationship between the stresses on people during emergencies, their aftereffects, and ways to minimize them. Details of those issues are beyond both the scope of this book and my own expertise,[16] so only the following brief outline is presented.

First, recognize the reality. Stress is a predictable, perfectly natural part of managing emergencies, and its aftereffects cannot be put aside without the individual's paying a penalty, often unrecognized until some time after the event. Second, accept the fact that not all managers will do well in situations where a lot of unfamiliar information must be integrated, decisions jointly derived, and their execution coordinated and then tracked in minimal time with the reputation — and perhaps the survival — of the organization at stake. One approach is to provide realistic management training and let those who do not perform adequately select themselves out. Another is to recognize those who *do* perform adequately and assign them to the emergency management team. Third, be sure a debriefing session is conducted very soon after each event. Those debriefings should include opportunities for individuals to discuss what worked, what the frustrations were, and what opportunities there are for improvement. Include someone with enough training to identify candidates for follow-up meetings with professionals, as well as an offer for no-fault, off-the-record meetings with a Critical Incident Stress management professional.

The most recent pages of this chapter have been discussing the management of the response phase—those things that must be done to stop and control the harm to people and physical damage to systems during a major disruptive event. It is now time to return to the means for dealing with those physical problems: ERTs.

One way to approach creating ERTs is to consider the problems that they will be expected to deal with. Here again, there is some good news. At the beginning of this chapter, the issue of threat evaluation resulted in an example of an earthquake scenario. This is a good time to introduce another scenario as an example of this approach to ERT creation, training, and supplies and equipment.

> *At 2 P.M. on a normal working day, people in our facility at the Business Park report unpleasant odors and watering eyes. This facility houses a call center for customer support and an order-taking and fulfillment center with product assembly, warehousing, and shipping operations. Within a few minutes, several people report nausea and difficulty with breathing. The facility's manager discovers that another company's facility upwind is releasing an unknown gas from an out-of-control chemical reaction. Public Safety Services order evacuation of the Business Park, and our facility's people move to our company's predetermined relocation area.*

While this example scenario is another good one for business unit managers to respond to with an impact assessment, it is included here to help readers think about creating, training, and equipping ERTs. Our facility in the Business Park has at least one neighbor capable of generating hazmat events. It also has many people in the customer service call center and order-taking and fulfillment areas. We can reasonably expect that the potential for incidents such as heart attacks and injuries is present. Without overinvesting in extensive research, that leads to providing the following training: CPR, basic first aid, first aid for respiratory distress, directing relocation or evacuations, handling hazmat events, and coordinating with public safety responders. Very briefly, that is how the training aspect can be approached, but there are a couple of items in that list for not-altogether-obvious reasons. One is CPR.

CPR is quickly and easily learned, involves beginners in the physical (and fun) aspects of training early in the process, is internationally recognized, and can be put to use anywhere at any time. Early in one's training, the sense of early accomplishment becomes real. That makes it a great way to start training ERT members. Another not-so-obvious inclusion was handling hazmat events.

"Handling" is not to be taken literally when training for hazmat events. For most ERT members, a brief introduction to hazmat events would include event recognition, isolating the source from the people to be protected (usually by shelter-in-place techniques), adding first aid training specifically matched to the probable substances, relocating the affected without contaminating others, and basic decontamination.

A note here about recruiting potential ERT members is appropriate. A quick survey of employees to determine who has had prior training and experience can uncover many people whose background shows that they are already motivated and save time and money in the training process. Appendix B of this chapter provides a list of ERT training options with some potential matches of threats to specific knowledge and skills.

Appendix C of this chapter provides a list of potential ERT supplies and equipment, but a caution is imperative: *Do not make equipment available that all ERT members are not yet trained to use.* A couple of illustrations may be useful here; one of the first things in good fire extinguisher training is when to retreat. In plain language, this means when to recognize that your extinguisher and skills are overmatched, and therefore to close the door and wait for the professional firefighters. Another instance is the use of tourniquets. Probably more harm than good has been done by hasty application of tourniquets in the field without adequate training. For that reason, in recent years tourniquets have been removed from most first aid kits available to minimally trained employees, and the same principle applies to ERTs. Add supplies and equipment to the team's gear as members become trained to use them.

At this point, we have discussed avoiding disasters applied to two of the three management levels that exist in most organizations. We began by discussing the need for policy-level (senior management) support, then dropped to the need for an internal response capability (ERTs). Middle management has a function to perform in avoiding disasters, too. Crisis management is the subject of the next chapter.

Appendix A: Threats-Hazards List

THREATS-HAZARDS

NATURAL HAZARDS

Avalanche
Cyclone—regionally, also: Hurricane or Typhoon
Drought
    Agricultural
    Urban
Earthquake
Epidemic—may also be terrorism
Firestorm
Floods
    Flash flooding
    River flooding
    Urban flooding
Hailstorm
Hurricane—regionally, also: Cyclone or Typhoon
Lahar
Landslide
Solar storm
Subsidence—may also be anthropogenic or accidental
Tornado
Tropical storm
Tsunami
Typhoon—regionally, also: Cyclone or Hurricane
Volcanic eruption
    Ash fall
    Pyroclastic flow
Wildland fire
    Wildland-urban intermix fire
Windstorm—regionally, also: Chinook, Foehn wind, Sandstorm, Sirocco, Williwaw

Winter storm
    Ice and snow
    Severe or Prolonged rain and wind

ANTHROPOGENIC, OR HUMAN-CAUSED, THREATS

Bomb incident
    Bomb threat
    Detonation—also, explosion
    Device found
Civil disorder—also, riot
Collateral damage
Cyber attacks—may also be terrorism related
Explosion—also, under Bomb incident, detonation
Extortion attempt
Fires (arson)
Funds missing
Kidnapping
Protests—Surrogates
Radioactive contamination
Subsidence—may also be naturally occurring or accidental
Terrorism
    Epidemic—may also be naturally occurring
    Cyber attack disrupting infrastructure
    Hazardous materials releases
    Transportation disruptions (see below)

ACCIDENTS, OR TECHNOLOGICAL THREATS

Building collapse
Cyber outages
Dam failure
Hazardous materials incidents
    Stationary source
    Transportation related
Infrastructure failures—see also Lifeline failures

Communications
Gas
Sewer
Water
Transportation (see below)
Information systems crashes
Lifeline failures — see Infrastructure failures
Major fire
Nuclear facility incident
Power failure
Subsidence — may be naturally occurring or human caused
Supply chain failure
Transportation accident
Air
Highway
Pipeline
Rail
Water

Appendix B: Emergency Response Team Training

General

The threats identified at most sites make it prudent to select and train Emergency Response Team members to develop these capabilities:

➤ Relocation or evacuation

➤ CPR and first aid

➤ Fighting incipient fires

➤ Damage control and hazardous materials control

➤ Work environment extrication and rescue

Specific

Relocation or Evacuation

Many threats point to scenarios involving relocation or evacuation: terrorist attacks,[17] hazardous materials incidents, fires, tornados, and earthquakes. It is advisable to train a pilot group for Emergency Response Team development, including relocation or evacuation of disabled people. Normal relocation or evacuation procedures include notifying, searching for, and removing those employees who do not have emergency duties from the impacted areas first. Relocation or evacuation as used here includes conducting people to an assembly area and accounting for persons there.

CPR and First Aid

Although these skills are valuable for almost all scenarios, they will most likely be used during earthquakes, tornados, fires, hazardous materials incidents, workplace violence, and individuals' medical emergencies. Especially in medical emergencies, time is of the essence; therefore, training to conduct rapid patient assessments is essential. Training should be as realistic as practical so that members know what to expect and will not hesitate when confronted with reality. An additional segment for first aid training in locations where the potential for building collapse is high (e.g., earthquake country and tornado alleys) is dealing with crush and penetrating injuries in both those areas; and where hurricanes occur, it is advisable to add basic nursing skills to use while waiting for delayed emergency responders.

Fighting Incipient Fires

Shirtsleeve fire fighting might be a better term. The basic concept is to stop fires while they are small, limiting damage and injuries from smoke and heat long before sprinkler heads open and add water damage. An important part of incipient fire suppression is understanding when a fire has grown beyond the limits of Emergency Response Team training and equipment. Fires after earthquakes and tornados will probably have to be attacked by Emergency Response Teams because broken water pipes can disable sprinklers, and fire departments must give priority in responses to life hazards at places such as schools and hospitals.

Building Damage and Hazardous Materials Control

In earthquakes, tornados, hurricanes, explosions, fires, and hazardous materials incidents, the ability to quickly shut down, isolate, and restore a building's internal systems can do these things:

1. Limit exposing employees to harm. Example: shutting down heating, ventilation, and air conditioning

(HVAC) to prevent taking in airborne chemicals approaching the facility's buildings.

2. Limit building damage. Example: shutting down sprinkler piping after an accident shears a sprinkler head.

3. Restore the business operational environment sooner. Example: restarting HVAC systems.

Working Environment Extrication and Rescue

After earthquakes and in more common accidents, it is necessary to have the ability to safely free and remove people who have been pinned or isolated . Using more than simple hand tools and improvisation is not contemplated.

Emergency Response Team Training Curriculum

To demonstrate cost effectiveness, two objectives should be adopted for pilot training: first, evaluate the fit of the proposed training with the corporation's style; second, identify ways to reduce exposures identified in the facility.

Relocation or Evacuation — 1.5 hours[18]

Emergency Response Team members should receive instruction in the following: reasons for relocation or evacuations, when relocation or evacuation is not a good idea, psychology of managing groups, safety during relocation or evacuation, selecting routes and alternate routes, assembly areas and alternatives, personnel accounting, and reporting. Course should include surveys and practice.

CPR — 4.0 hours

Students should learn techniques to respond to a victim with respiratory or cardiac arrest or an obstructed airway. Course should include videos, lectures, handouts, and practice sessions.

First Aid—4.0 hours

Team members should be trained to treat severe bleeding, sprains, strains, and fractures. Where teams can have prolonged waits for transportation (during windstorms, earthquakes, and flooding, as well as in remote areas), the course should include patient care for more than a day. Training must include self-protection against blood-borne pathogens. The course should utilize videos, lectures, handouts, and practice using the supplies and equipment that should be used in actual emergencies.

Fighting Incipient Fires—2.0 hours

Team members should be trained to fight incipient stage fires. Course should include the following:

1. Fire chemistry—why it burns.

2. Fire behavior—how it extends.

3. Safe extinguisher use.

4. When to retreat.

Course should utilize videos, demonstrations, and practices.

Damage Assessment and Damage Control—1.5 hours

Team members should be instructed in locating essential systems shutoffs, when they may be used, how to activate them, and how to restore them. Team members should be trained in operating their HVAC systems, electrical systems, and annunciator panels and in reporting damage.

Course should utilize handouts, systems' plans, as-built drawings, survey tours, and practices.

Working Environment Extrication and Rescue—2.5 hours

Team members should be instructed in safety for both rescuers and victims. Team members should learn to search systematically for missing people. Team members should also receive instruction in victims' and rescuers' protection during disentanglement and removal. Team members should learn to utilize basic on-hand equipment such as car jacks, wrenches, hammers, pry bars, and furniture as cribbing. Students should learn basic leverage and how they can use available equipment safely in an emergency.

Course should use handouts, videos, manikins, site tours, and practices.

Appendix C: A List of Potential Emergency Response Team Supplies and Equipment

Caution! Do not make equipment available that all Emergency Response Team members are not yet trained to use.

Notes

1. The quantities are recommended for a cabinet supplying two three-person Emergency Response Teams serving an average of 15 people per team.

2. An allowance for training is also required and should be worked out with the Trainers you will be using.

3. Wherever a brand name appears, its equivalent may be substituted.

Personal Protective Equipment

Personal Protective Equipment (PPE) for use by Emergency Response Team (ERT) members.

6	Hard-hats, with organization's logo and "EMERGENCY RESPONSE TEAM" stencil, plus face shield (clear plastic, to stop airborne body fluids)
18	Dust masks
6	Pairs of work gloves with leather palms
6	Hat-mounted lights with spare batteries and a spare bulb
6	Identification vests, with organization's logo and "EMERGENCY RESPONSE TEAM" in high-contrast stencil, not less than 4" vertical letters, front and back
2	Adult CPR air-exchange prevention masks
15 pair	Examination gloves

Medical

2	Carry-on bags, for this kit. Cordura nylon or equivalent, in shoulder bag/backpack convertible style, with organization's logo
2 bottles	Acetaminophen, 325-mg tabs, 100 tabs/bottle (Tylenol or equivalent)
2 boxes	Adhesive compress, 1" × 3" Band-Aid or equivalent dressing/bandages, 100/box
4	Bandage and dressing, pressure, 5" × 9", Carlyle, or Surgipad type
2	Bandage shears, plastic handles, stainless blades, blunt tip, serrated edges, approximately 7 1/4"
12 rolls	Bandage, conforming 2" × 5 yards/roll; Kling, or stretch-gauze type
8 rolls	Bandages, elastic, 3" × 5 yards; Ace, Cobans, or equivalent
6	Bandages, triangular muslin, approximately 40", with safety pins
3	Blankets, approximately 70% wool, approximately 62" × 90"
10	Blankets, Mylar or equivalent, survival-type
10	Dressings, 5" × 9" Surgipad ABD or equivalent
8	Dressings, Eye pad, approximately 2 1/2" × 1 1/2"
100	Examination gloves, boxed
2 bottles	Eye irrigation fluid, Dacriose or equivalent, approximately 4 oz., in squeeze bottles
2	Forceps, pair, splinter approx 4"
2	Hydrogen peroxide 16-oz. bottles.
4	Splints, cardboard, adult arm, disposable, approximately 18"
4	Splints, cardboard, adult leg, disposable, approximately 24"

2 pkgs	Sponges, gauze 4″ × 4″ approximately 8-ply, bulk packaged, 200/pkg
2	squirt bottles glucose
20	Tags, casualty treatment and identification, MetTag or equivalent
4 rolls	Tape, water-resistant 1″ × 5 yard/roll
8	Tongue depressors
20	Towelettes, zephiran chloride or equivalent, disposable

Survival

24 liters	water, 2 liters per container enough for 2 liters per person daily for 3 days
2 bottles	Water purification tablets
30	Meals, ready-to-eat (MREs)

Damage Control and Rescue

2	Buckets 16 quart
4 rolls	Duct Tape (2″ × 60 yards/roll)
12	Garbage bags, large, industrial-duty
1	Hacksaw
10	Spare hacksaw blades
10	Light sticks, white, high intensity, 30 minutes
20	Light sticks, white, low intensity, 8 hour
1	Litter, folding Reeves-type
1 roll	Plastic sheeting (20 ft × 25 ft/roll, 4 mil.)
1 pair	Pliers, vice grip or equivalent (10″)
2	Halligan tools, 30″ rescue tool
2	Pry bars (burglar-approved)
1 coil	Rope (100 ft./coil)
2	Screwdrivers, flat-blade, large
2	Screwdriver, Phillips, sized to match facility's hardware
1	Sledge, 2 lb., to match Halligan tool

Deferred Delivery

The following supplies and equipment should not be placed in the cabinets until the Emergency Response Teams are trained to use them:

20	Applicators, cotton-tipped, 6"
1	Collar, extrication stiff plastic adult/regular
2	Hazardous materials control and cleanup kits
3	Sand bags, 3 lb. vinyl covered
2	Sphygmomanometers, aneroid, adult
2	Splints, inflatable full leg adult
2	Splints, inflatable, full arm adult
2	Stethoscopes, single head
4	Tourniquets, Penrose (do not substitute a generic brand), approximately 1" × 18"

Chapter 3

Manage It or . . .

. . . or else it will manage you. It's true.

Without a Crisis Management Team (CMT) and its support in place, a major disruptive event is likely to take on a life of its own, driving your company into decisions that will negatively effect plans for a bright future. Worse, it can lead to that graveyard spiral aviators know about. Event becomes crisis; crisis becomes disaster; and on down. Over the longer term, resources for expansion are consumed,[1] employees being groomed for promotion leave,[2] and the confidence of investors, regulators, potential partners, and customers is shaken.

Some readers have probably been thinking that crisis management is such an important element in avoiding disasters that it should have been discussed before this. Important as it is, without the elements we discussed in the previous chapter—senior management's commitment and connection and an internal response capability for major events—the capability for crisis management will be severely limited. In any case, the ability to deal with business functions during a major event is the second part of the fifth of the 10 principles that are essential to keep disruptive events from growing—and thus to avoid disasters.

■ CRISIS MANAGEMENT TEAM

In this section I describe the need for the organization and functioning of a CMT. At first, it will seem a lot like the Emergency Management Team that supports emergency response in the field. That's understandable. In fact, until recently most professionals had difficulty differentiating between managing business continuity during a crisis and managing the field response, or they envisioned the way to do it as something like "changing the watch" as different people move into the same positions or as different skills are brought to bear—as though there were some moment in time when an organization abruptly switches from managing the response to managing business continuity. I believe that concept is in error.

Here is the reasoning for having two distinct teams whose operations overlap in time. First, a company that waits to address issues of business continuity until after the fires are out, water leaks are stopped, and most of the other dangers are controlled is likely to discover that those things take a lot longer than anticipated. In addition, the company's employees, customers, investors, and regulating agencies will want to know what is being done about business continuity long before that. Second, issues of business continuity are most effectively and efficiently addressed by middle management's mindset, resources, and familiarity with corporate goals and objectives. Third (and perhaps not last in importance), the consequences of delaying action on the many business issues that need attention during a major event can severely impact the company's bottom line. Restoring production to keep customers happy (and maybe to keep customers, period) and to demonstrate that yours is a prepared, well-run organization requires action before the business segment of the evening news comes on. In short, we need two teams.

The CMT should be quite different from the team supporting field emergency response. What they are called is less important than that their roles are understood and that their names do not jar the corporate culture. Having laid these concepts as foundation, it is time to repeat an essential truism about teams.

> However carefully an organization goes through the steps, and however well drawn its emergency plans are, it is the management teams' proficiency, achieved through practice, that can achieve success and efficiency and ultimately determine the organization's reputation when a threat materializes that might become a major event.

As with the previous team, the characteristics of the CMT remain the following:

1. Selecting members to bring together knowledge and expertise who can deal with a major disruptive event threatening the organization's ability to perform its mission.

2. Developing the team's ability to gather information about what is happening quickly.

3. Training the team to determine which team members need that information and efficiently share it among them.

4. Ensuring that the team either

   a. Decides on an immediate course of action for a given item (probably 8 out of 10 items will be managed this way), or

   b. Bucks the issue and its analysis upstairs to senior
   management for a decision.

5. Developing the team's proficiency in identifying and directing resources necessary to carry out those decisions.

6. Monitoring how effectively those decisions are being carried out and adjusting directions as necessary.

Emergency management teams should perform numerous adjunct functions, but these six functions are the essential ones to keep an event from entering that graveyard spiral leading to a crater — provided the team's proficiency is maintained. The next thing to think about is what form the team's organization should assume. In other words, what framework best defines the lines of authority and communication for the team?

   If your organization chooses to continue using the Incident Command System model described and illustrated to this point (although there are other models, as I shall point out next), the addition of two more functions should be seriously considered because of their critical importance in contemporary businesses. They are human resources and information/telecommunications services. Please see Figure 3.1, which uses the Incident Command System model purely for illustration.

   Although the previous chapter outlined two models, for *this* team there is little advantage to be gained by using a structure that mimics that of the field response teams (Emergency Response Teams) and governmental emergency responders, mainly police or fire and rescue services. Therefore, I recommend using a structure that facilitates the ways in which the reader's organization usually operates. In other words, the structure of your CMT will probably look a lot like your company's current organization chart.

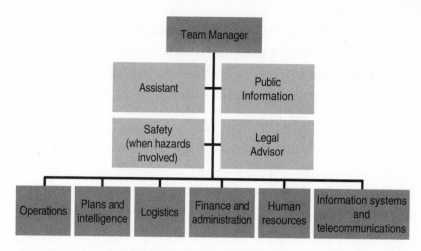

Figure 3.1 Crisis Management Team organization chart modified to reflect importance of direct human resources and information systems control *Note.* Manager's span of control is at maximum.

Whatever model you use, it needs to be connected *above, below,* and *laterally.* The connection *above* is to senior management. There are two principal purposes for that connection. First, senior management is automatically in line to monitor impacts on business operations. Second, the CMT can buck certain decisions along with its analysis of them up to senior management. Candidates for one of those "certain decisions" include any situation not covered by policy and any situation in which too much is at stake for middle management to deal with.

The *lateral* connection goes to the Emergency Management Team so that situation reports coming from Emergency Response Teams with information that will impact the company's business functions reach the CMT promptly. There is a danger here — that CMT members, many of whom came up through the ranks, will understandably try to direct field Emergency Response Teams, either directly or through the Emergency Management Team. Although understandable, it is bad practice and is very likely to lead to confusion at a time when the organization's leadership needs to speak clearly, using one line of authority, and needs a concerted effort to overcome the inevitable excitement and emotion that contribute to confusion.

The connection below goes to the business units and gets estimates about the severity of impacts that the event is having on them. The relative severities are important because at least temporarily, a major event will result in too few resources pursuing too many problems. The CMT will need that information to prioritize its reactions and assignment of resources.

Whatever model is used, some supporting functions are needed, and this is an opportunity to discuss those. The requirement to set up the CMT's venue, usually called an Emergency Operations Center by government agencies but without much name standardization in the private sector (though I will call it a Crisis Management Center),[3] is obvious. I have seen CMTs function adequately in dedicated high-tech facilities resembling military command centers, luxurious conference rooms, employees' break areas, tents, and parking lots. Wherever the venue is, it needs people to set it up. Less obvious until a CMT has occupied it for a while is the requirement to sustain it in reasonable operating condition. A support crew is needed around the clock.

There are also supporting specialized functions that need to be inside the Crisis Management Center or very nearby: public relations, legal-regulatory liaison, information systems and communications, and safety wherever there are hazardous processes to be controlled. In the classic military or Incident Command System organization chart, they are attached to the stem leading downward from the team manager, showing that they are supporting staff functions, not in the direct line of authority and thus not authorized to issue orders. The Incident Command System or

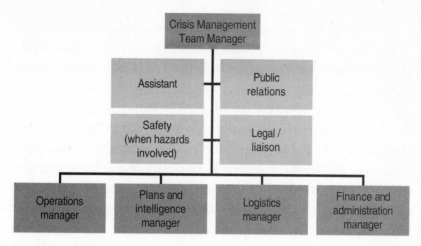

Figure 3.2 Incident Command System organization chart modified to provide staff assistance.

Emergency Management Team model would thus be modified into something like that shown in Figure 3.2.

In models where some support expertise is contracted out, these are also added to the stem from the team manager. Government agencies typically use the Red Cross in this way for their sheltering expertise, and engineering resource management may appear in earthquake, tornado, and hurricane areas. The principle can also be used to good effect in private-sector Crisis Management Centers.

As with an Emergency Management Team, the manager's principal task is to keep the CMT doing integrated management. The sharing of information, discussion, and joint decision making are at first very difficult for most organizations because the various disciplines are usually accustomed to dealing with business decisions in a stovepipe or silo management environment. However, in a crisis most situations are going to impact several parts of the organization—if not immediately, then after the decision is implemented. In an example that I experienced personally, a loss of telecommunications bandwidth meant less-than-usual capacity, so the decision to cut off one or another division of the organization had to allow for forthcoming events that were critical to the company's bottom line. Another example involved an extensive fire that cut off access to a trust department's vault shortly before a high-revenue transaction based on an instrument in that vault had to be executed. Liaison resources were directed to that situation, the instrument was retrieved from an area secured as a crime scene, and the transaction took place as scheduled.[4] In both cases, the shared information and joint decision making—integrated emergency management—produced good results and prevented millions of dollars more in costs.

■ CRISIS MANAGEMENT IN SMALL-TO MEDIUM-SIZED COMPANIES

At about this point in the development of the previous chapter, the subject of small- to medium-sized companies was introduced. Readers may be wondering about whether the roles just discussed can be managed by anything but a large corporation. The short answer is yes.

Medium-sized and even small companies and other organizations can use the same steps to avoid disasters, including the same crisis management roles just outlined. The principal difference is that for small organizations individuals will probably fill more than one role. However, because that is how small organizations often must operate, the difference should not intimidate a policy maker or manager who understands what is at risk.

For small- and medium-sized companies, once the reasoning that leads to multiple roles has been thought through, policy makers and managers thinking about avoiding disasters will find that the same functions have to be performed as in the largest ones. At that point, the key becomes prioritizing because the number of people and time to train them will not be available. Therefore, thinking it through beforehand and assigning priorities to what must be done and in what sequence is vital for small- and medium-sized organizations.

■ QUICK SITUATION ASSESSMENT

Here is a generic list of priority issues for quickly getting essential knowledge during crises:

1. Establish a source on the ground.
   a. Be sure of the name and position of your contact. Agree on a dependable way to communicate, and agree on an alternate communications path.
   b. Ask whether your contact is in a safe position. If not, instruct the caller to move to safety.
   c. If in doubt about the contact (bona fide? stable? adequate overview?), get a trusted individual on the scene.
2. If anyone is dead, injured, or missing, be sure that help is en route.
3. Confirm that the facility's local Crisis Management Center and emergency management team are being set up.
4. Determine whether production[5] will be compromised, and determine percentage lost and downtime.
5. Determine whether local issues may compromise your company's credibility.
6. Activate your CMT and pass those items along.

Especially for small companies, adopting a framework for crisis management as close as is practical to the company's structure for managing normal operations will simplify training or rapid adaptation when a threat becomes an event. The goal is the same for all organizations: to stop the graveyard spiral. The method is also the same: integrated emergency management. Now, let us discuss a place to do that: the Crisis Management Center.

■ CRISIS MANAGEMENT CENTER ESSENTIALS

I have been present where CMTs have functioned adequately in venues ranging from a dedicated facility with state-of-the-art electronics and graphics to a tent with chalkboards on tables and pretransistor telephones. However, they all must perform these basic functions:

➤ Provide a place for the CMT to assemble[6]

➤ Provide means rapidly to obtain, store, and integrate situation information

➤ Facilitate the CMT's assessment of developments

➤ Facilitate exchange of specialized knowledge and expertise among CMT members, subject-matter experts, and decision makers located elsewhere to determine how to deal with developments

➤ Provide means to obtain resources, direct and monitor actions, and record events

A reasonably comprehensive list of Crisis Management Center supplies and equipment is provided in the Appendix A of this chapter. Having discussed the Crisis Management Center, where the CMT works, the next subject for additional discussion is the CMT itself.

■ THE CRISIS MANAGEMENT TEAM

The key person is the team's manager. Ideally, the manager should be higher in the organization's hierarchy than anyone else in the room, but at least equally important is the ability to keep his or her own excitement under control in critical situations and transmit a sense of calm competency to others in the room. There are several reasons why individuals should be selected for that ability: First, people who are overexcited do not think clearly, and judgment is critically important in the high-stakes game of corporate crisis management; second, many others outside the Crisis Management Center will be making their own assessments of the CMT's (as it reflects the company's) competence to deal with disruptive events from the tone and level of what they hear and, with the increasing use of real-time screen presentations, from what they have placed before them; third, managers with the capacity for self-evaluation are highly desirable. My experiences as both first point of contact and as supervisor in Crisis Management Centers and air traffic control centers have highlighted the impacts of fatigue on both time lags and quality of judgment — often without the individual's awareness. In plain language, the high data rates, unfamiliar situations, and high stakes of a Crisis Management Center provide numerous opportunities for bad decisions, with unintended consequences that can exacerbate them afterward.

Fortunately, there are reliable ways to help select the people who will be assigned to a CMT. Most younger managers are confident of their ability to meet the challenge and will seek the opportunity to participate. Most senior managers have had several opportunities to evaluate themselves on the way to becoming a senior manager. They know whether they will work well there or not. Those who demur are probably the best judges of their capabilities in that environment and should be believed. After self-selection comes the opportunity to listen to the nominee's supervisor, who can be valuable, unproductive, or misleading. That uncertainty relates to the relatively short tenures of the incumbents in many management positions, which should be factored into supervisors' ratings when known. Probably the strongest assessment tool is observation during CMT training. The best training is an exercise in which a realistic scenario is given the CMT in an interactive game of team versus wanna-be disaster. A caution here: Just one exercise may not provide enough observations to decide on a given nominee, because keeping one's cool can be learned. This, of course, is one powerful reason for giving the CMT training exercises (i.e., opportunities to rehearse).

The positions assigned to CMT members should be matched to the functions to be performed. I use a two-dimensional grid with existing positions on one of the axes and crisis management functions on the other.[7] Table 3.1 is a very abbreviated example of a functions-versus-responsibility grid. In concept, it is pretty simple: Across the top, write your company's business units; and down the left side, write the functions to be performed during major disruptive events. P is for primary responsibility (use only one P for each function); S is for support to the primary. There are additional explanations under the grid.

In the blocks where there is an existing match, place the letter P (for primary responsibility). For example, people issues (casualties, family assistance) are almost always assigned to the representative from human resources (HR); for a second

Table 3.1   Functions-versus-Responsibility Grid

	Responsible Business Units					
Functions	Human Resources	Finance	Facilities and Security	Information Systems and Telecommunications	Logistics and Purchasing	Public Relations
Casualty management	P		S	S		S
Expense tracking		P			S	
Employee relocation and evacuation	S		S		P	

example, tracking the extraordinary expenditures disruptive events cause usually goes to finance's representative.

Readers who have reasoned that if there is a P designating primary responsibility, then there must be another designator related to the same function, are correct. In the first example, the HR representative will require support (S) at least from the individual managing the Emergency Response Teams dealing with casualties in the field, which is often the facilities-security representative, so a second letter, S, goes where people issues and facilities intersect. In the second example, finance's representative will get much of that function's needed information from the logistics-purchasing representative, so an S was placed in that intersection. For many primary responsibilities, there will be more than one supporting manager. Looking again at the HR example, the need for HR to communicate with families will usually put an additional S at both the information systems—telecommunications and the public relations intersections.

A list of many of the CMT functions and brief explanations of what those functions do appears in Appendix B to this chapter along with a larger grid showing how they might be assigned. "Might" is the operative word. Readers understand their own organizations well enough to assign functions to managers with matching aptitudes and interests. Adapting that grid to match your company's reality is likely to be necessary and therefore is encouraged. If you find the number of positions or functions overwhelming compared to the numbers of your company's managers, be assured that this means only that some managers will have to take on more than one role, and the key to managing becomes prioritizing.

An essential responsibility for *every* manager is keeping a record of incoming information, actions taken, and outgoing communications. These logs may be your own and your company's best defense when the lawyers almost inevitably become involved.

Additional reassurance: your company's Crisis Management Center need not be activated by an all-or-nothing toggle switch. I recommend three levels of activation.

1. Low
   ➤ Plans and Intelligence monitors developments and collects data.
   ➤ Activate communication systems.
   ➤ Alert other CMT members to remain available and in touch.

2. Medium
   ➤ Manager of Crisis Management Center determines which additional functions to activate and requests that senior management designate an executive as representative.
   ➤ Purchasing and Logistics begins alerting suppliers.

3. High
   ➤ All hands and systems at work.

Fairly detailed information about structure for two of the usual three management layers[8] has been provided, and you may feel that there is an absence of detail for the top layer, or senior management. Indeed, we do not yet have the three layers playing together. Chapter 4 addresses that and other issues of interest to senior executives.

Before going on to Step 6, a brief review may be in order. This chapter first addressed the second part of Step 5: a middle-management CMT that compliments Chapter 3's Emergency Management Team, which supports the Emergency Response (field) Teams. We discussed the CMT's purposes, workable frameworks, connections, member-selection processes, internal functions, and how they can be assigned. We are now ready to move on to the Step 6: developing business continuity plans.

■ STEP 6: PLAN DEVELOPMENT

We begin with another review. The plan for a given organization is likely to involve more than one strategy, and some business units will require different strategies at different times, as was illustrated by Chapter 2's example of paycheck production before or after payday. Let us begin by acknowledging that *business continuity* implies zero apparent downtime, which is going to be overkill in many situations. To review, the possibilities are business continuity, quick restoration (usually before the next business day), and recovery, which may take a few working days. Please note that the pace of the business unit's operations sets the pace for its recovery. Think of a huge mining operation with large amounts of ore piled up waiting for transport—a situation very different from the trading floor of a stock exchange at the opening bell.

➤ Developing a Plan

The process of developing a plan, in general, goes in this sequence:

1. List the units' business functions.

2. Determine which are critical to the company's mission.[9]

3. Match them to appropriate strategies.

4. Determine the essential elements to operate the functions.

5. Choose ways to put the elements together within the strategies' time constraints.

6. Find and then list resources that match the ways you chose.

7. Contract in advance with the resources that will be needed quickly.

8. Rehearse putting the resources and essential elements together and conducting the business functions.

9. Make the necessary adjustments.

10. Rehearse again.

> Involve those who must implement the plan with every step!

There are several good reasons for the above admonition and its emphasis here.

➤ While the business units' managers have seen one or two scenarios during the risk analysis, their subordinates usually do the actual work. To be certain that a critical business function is not overlooked, check your understanding of the unit's functions and determine which are critical to the company's mission with those doing the work.

➤ When the plan is implemented, the people who will become its implementers must be familiar with it. It needs to be written using their terminology.

➤ Their buy-in is essential as a matter of good management practice. Without it, unintended consequences are almost guaranteed.

➤ They are the ones thoroughly familiar with the esential elements to operate the business functions (though you may have to help the worker bees articulate them).

Having emphasized that point, let's go back to examine the 10 items on that list and add some explanatory supplements.

Number 1: List the units' business functions. In the business unit of a bank that is a branch office, tellers receive money — one of their functions. A different business unit of the same bank is its international currency trading office, which must determine the correct monetary exchange rates — one of its functions. The bank's purchasing group buys paper clips — one of its functions.

Number 2: Determine which functions are critical to the mission. Back to the bank. Tellers taking in money are probably critical to a branch's mission, and so is knowing the correct monetary exchange rates; but determining whether they are critical is not to be determined by we who plan. At this point, the what-if scenarios can really help get the business units' managers and their implementers involved.

They will determine which are the mission-critical business functions.

Paper clips, anyone?

Number 3: Match the functions to one of the three appropriate strategies. Because this is a hypothetical bank existing only on these pages, I choose to make its trading function a 24-hour, 7-days per week (24-7) operation with very high monetary volume (billions per quarter). Which brings us to essential elements.

Number 4: Determine the elements that are essential to operate the functions. To simplify, using our bank's currency trading office, the essential elements are traders, telecommunications linkages, information systems (processing and displays), and transaction recording. To improve understanding, you should do the same mental exercise for any operation with which you are thoroughly familiar. It provides engaging mental exercise, and everything can be used—from one's avocation (a model club's holiday displays or a neighborhood barbecue) through a must-succeed professional effort (modernize an air traffic control system or keep an auto body shop competitive).

Number 5: Choose ways to put the elements together within the strategies' time constraints. Because the trading office in our hypothetical bank is 24-7, with very high monetary stakes, this planner will recommend isolated parallel information-systems processing and parallel telecommunications paths, with physically separated standby displays and transaction-recording capability.

The word "relative" becomes important here. Relative to other strategies, the costs for those recommendations are certainly going to be higher. However, relative to the lost revenue from an outage of more than a few minutes, those same costs are low. By now you are no doubt thinking of the most essential element: the traders.

Can traders be duplicated, too? In a sense, perhaps they can. Because ours is a 24-7 operation, there must be shifts. Can we devise a subsystem that rapidly gets the off-duty traders to an alternate work site with the duplicated systems? For planners and implementers working their way through these issues, thinking outside the box pays dividends. Don't expect a thinking breakthrough for every issue, but when one comes, it saves — and not just money.

Number 6: Find and then list resources that match the ways you chose. Alternate work sites exist to be contracted for in advance of need. Alternate telecommunications providers abound. Additional displays and transaction storage are manifold and inexpensive. Repeat the exercise until a resources list of everything needed to match the chosen ways to keep operating or restore critical business functions exists.

Number 7: Contract with the providers of those resources that will be needed quickly. Advance contracts are important because the line for scarce resources will be long when a regional emergency arises (think "natural disaster"). In addition, resources coming from afar will be commensurately (and sometimes outrageously) expensive.

Number 8: Rehearse putting the resources and essential elements together and conducting the business functions. Although it seems redundant to emphasize this again, I know several companies that have gone to great expenses of time, money, and effort to produce plans that remain untested. Rehearse, exercise, or practice. Whatever your organization calls it, you will be very glad you did it when threat becomes reality and tries to push your outfit into that graveyard spiral.

Number 9: Make the necessary adjustments. At the end of every rehearsal (exercise or practice), collect the participants' lessons learned and use them to improve the plan and the next practice. More on that later in this chapter, but for now think of it as an important element in involving the implementers.

Number 10: Rehearse again.

Having reviewed and expanded that 10-item guideline, it is time to return to the large-scale 10 steps to avoiding disasters.

■ STEPS 7 AND 8: AWARENESS AND TRAINING, AND MAINTAINING AND EXERCISING PLANS

➤ Training Management Teams to Use the Plan

Step 7 in our 10-step sequence is to create awareness and training programs. Step 8 is maintaining and exercising business continuity plans. Both steps logically link together, and doing one step almost inevitably achieves at least part of the other. One reason is that training programs, through the informal communications webs (grapevines) existing in almost all organizations, will create awareness as soon as team recruiting, selection, and training come to light. Ways to leverage those processes will be explored in Chapter 10. Another reason is that one of the principal motivations for exercising *is* training. In fact, when discussing training for responding to or managing disruptive events, exercising (practicing practical application of the principles) is very effective and the most efficient and intellectually engaging (fun) way to train. Anything that is fun is going to get favorable grapevine circulation. Yet another reason why awareness, training, plan maintenance, and exercising are logically bound together is that the second principal reason for exercising is plan maintenance. I realize that the usual approach describes one purpose of management exercises as *testing* the plan, but ultimately a test highlights actions that are needed to keep it effective (i.e., maintenance).

Considerable awareness will already have been achieved during the first five steps. At the operational level, the Emergency Response Teams and their management support, the Emergency Management Team, will not have gone unnoticed. Internal memoranda and house newsletters (including in-house e-mail equivalents) can be used to announce implementation of the company's disaster avoidance effort, with later reinforcement by noting milestones and achievements. The Emergency Response Teams' training exercises provide opportunities to capture excellent visuals, and those can be tied to Emergency Response Team recruiting. Depending on the corporate culture, opportunities to train Emergency Response Teams in conjunction with local governments' first responders, notably the fire and rescue services, can have a number of good effects: recognition, free training, shared expectations when they work together on a major emergency, and easy cooperation during more common events such as on-site medical emergencies.

At the middle management level, the nomination and selection of candidates for the CMT will have gained similar notice. Again, management training exercises (more on exercises as training later in this chapter) will have had similar effects on awareness. There are also management-training opportunities for corporate middle managers through public agencies.[10] I recommend the Federal Emergency Management Agency's (FEMA) Emergency Management Institute courses in integrated emergency management. Private sector managers can attend and bring a much-needed familiarity with corporate (i.e., community economic drivers') needs, bringing nongovernment managers' expertise and perspective while filling key roles in mock-community teams, especially in the mitigation and recovery course.[11] There are also private-sector course opportunities, which will be listed with more detail in Chapter 11.

Some readers may assume that there is little need for awareness, training, and exercising at the senior management and policy levels because that is where this all started—with senior management's commitment and connection in Chapter 2—but that is seldom true. Even senior managers who understand how much is at risk need memory refreshers. In fact, the number and intensity of distractions at the policy level may be greater than those that middle managers face. For that reason, including senior executives in exercises—in fact, creating an exercise for them—is likely to help keep the company's disaster-avoidance program on track by reinforcing that essential commitment and connection. Senior management should be briefed as major milestones are achieved at other levels: when the pilot Emergency Response Team is established, when Emergency Management Team and CMT members are selected, when they are trained, and so on. In most organizations, the board of directors and senior management expect training goals and timelines to be sent to them soon after a program is authorized, so reinforcement should take care of itself, but the previous reminder was added "in case." As we have reached some basic discussion of exercises, the time has come to discuss them in more detail.

There is easily enough content on the purpose, creation, and implementation of response and management training exercises to fill another book, so this book will continue to avoid miring readers in detail and concentrate on trying to get principles into the readers' hands.

➤ Exercises Train People While Testing The Plan

There are four reasons for exercises. Two are often explicitly stated as exercise goals, and they are to *test* the Plan and to *train* the implementers. One reason that is sometimes verbally admitted, but less often written, is to reinforce acceptance of the whole process by the implementers. The fourth reason is almost always present, but is never committed to writing and is spoken of only when the project's planners are alone with the doors shut. It is to reinforce acceptance by senior management. There will be more discussion of that fourth reason later in this book, but for now let's return to the first three reasons.

Testing the plan includes but is not limited to checking understandability for the implementers, confirming integration among management functions, validating the sequence of the plan's steps reflected in team members' checklists, assessing the flow between management phases,[12] and determining the adequacy of resources. Training the plan's implementers includes at least plan familiarization, orientation of the crisis management venue ("Welcome to your Crisis Management Center!"), crisis management structure introduction, role validation, feedback collection, and just plain rehearsing—demystifying what at first will seem strange. Acceptance will result from two endeavors: getting the players' feedback and letting them see it become part of the plan (plan maintenance—part of Step 8), together with their realization that the plan will work. The latter is also the key to senior management's acceptance.

The separation of the terms *testing* and *training* is important. Putting people into a different environment—their Crisis Management Center—and using a different organizational structure almost guarantees stress. Telling them that they are about to be *tested,* with all that that implies before peers and seniors, need not be added to the mix. For that reason, emphasize and reinforce to the Team that only the plan will be tested—with the explicit objective of collecting their recommendations for changes. What will the team be doing? *Training.*

My introduction to exercising for management teams

goes as follows: "In a training environment, errors are understandable and expected. Nobody's professional reputation is on the line during an exercise. Although the scenarios and exercise environment are as realistic as we can make them, there will be no real casualties, no real production interrupted, no market share lost, and no real impact on your company's stock prices. In short, relax and learn. And keep a written Lessons Learned List so we can improve the plan using the ideas you will have during this exercise." You are encouraged to use or modify this speech to kick off your own exercises.

Exercises can answer several exciting issues:

➤ Were the planning assumptions giving priorities to one function over others correct?

➤ Are the cues for coordinating among team members right?

➤ Were the expectations of support from the business units not represented on the team and "outside" organizations realistic?

➤ Were the right individuals picked as members?

➤ Do the team members who will be the plan's implementers have the confidence that comes from rehearsal?

➤ Can senior management be told with confidence what protections the plan affords?

Selecting an exercise's goal and objectives is critical. The goal should a combination of your organization's mission statement with the recognized threats to continued operations. Here is an example for a tabletop, or familiarization, exercise:

Goal: *Increase the disaster-management capability of the organization by familiarizing participants with information-flow requirements during a major disruptive event and with how the plan facilitates that flow.*

Here is an example for a functional, or interactive, exercise:

Goal: *Increase the company's disaster-management capability through practice for Crisis Management Center decision makers and staff in integrated emergency management and in responding to the requirements to maintain or restore mission critical business operations.*

An exercise's objectives are subordinate to its goal and should be upgraded as progress in training and testing goes forward. This means that the objectives for the follow-up exercises for the same team will be written to further develop the team's capabilities. A few words of caution are appropriate; be sure that each objective is feasible, and keep the total number of objectives low enough that everyone can keep them in mind during the training. Here is an example for a functional (interactive) exercise to be conducted in the Crisis Management Center:

Objectives:

➤ Conduct the training with minimal impact on normal business activities.

➤ Review participants' roles in the Business Continuity Plan.

➤ Familiarize decision makers and staff with Crisis Management Center operations.

➤ Practice integrated emergency management decision making.

➤ Produce Lessons Learned Lists to improve all aspects of the organization's emergency management.

There are three kinds of exercises: tabletop exercises, functional exercises, and full-scale (or field) exercises. For functional exercises, there are two variations: scripted and interactive. We shall discuss their differences shortly. It is important that every manager who participates be told before each exercise starts that achievement of the objectives is the reason for conducting the exercise; therefore, when the objectives are reached, the exercise will end.

Chapter 10 offers some additional recommendations, but for now it is important when setting objectives to know that they are the bases for the scenario.

No doubt that last statement may seem strange, but it is important and true. A list of realistic scenarios that reflect real dangers to the company can be developed by reviewing the threats that were assessed as both high probability and high impact. Too often, a scenario unrelated to the high probability-high impact threat category is picked because it seemed intriguing or because someone said, "I always wanted to see if . . ." Such a scenario might work, but it must provide opportunities to achieve the exercise's objectives *and* to determine whether they are achieved. Scenarios to avoid are those that are highly improbable. A scenario that begins, "As the terrorist frogmen parachute into the refinery's oil tanks . . . ," will turn off people needed to participate in an exercise, not to mention their bosses who must approve their diversion from their business unit's principal work.

➤ Familiarization Exercises

There is a set and order of events that lead to successful *tabletop* exercises:

➤ Preparation of the Emergency Management Team

➤ A setting that facilitates training (usually a classroom with a seminar layout)

➤ Realistic expectations by the trainers (Exercise Controller and Simulation Group) about participants' study of the plan (very few will have time)

➤ Realization that participants' minimal prior study will require creative effort by the trainers to use exercise events to help the participants learn their parts of the plan

➤ Division of the exercise into parts to reach the objectives

➤ Incorporation of participants' feedback into future exercises.

Usually, only one tabletop exercise is required to familiarize participants with their parts of the plan and to lead them to an elementary understanding of how their parts work with other participants' parts. The next step is functional exercising.

➤ Teamwork Rehearsal Exercises

Several functional exercises will usually be required before senior management and the emergency-preparedness program manager are assured that the emergency management team and alternate team members are adequately prepared for actual major emergencies. The responsible manager will have to gauge the rate at which exercises should be presented and the interval between them. There are no absolute rules about those times, but some factors are the time required for senior management to receive the report and absorb the lessons learned from each exercise, other vital activities in the organization's business cycle (e.g., budgeting), and the need to incorporate changed requirements.

Conducting functional exercises requires

➤ Advancing objectives

➤ Involving the management team in selecting the next exercise's objectives

➤ Using more sophisticated scenarios to match the advancing objectives

➤ Conducting the exercise in the Crisis Management Center

➤ Establishing a separate space for the Simulation Group (after functional exercises become interactive)

➤ Using the communications that will be used during actual emergencies

➤ Pretraining the Simulation Group

The first functional exercise is usually conducted from a script of events to be introduced in sequence, although the Exercise Controller determines the times at which they are introduced, being guided by the rate at which the team is learning. Exercises are terminated when one of three situations occur:

1. The objectives are achieved.

2. An actual major emergency occurs that will require team members.

3. The time allotted for the exercise expires. For exercises early in their evolution, approximately two hours is recommended, including a period for review and analysis. For later exercises, three hours of actual

exercising before the review and analysis period is usually optimal.

The emergency management team's alternate members usually sit behind or next to their primary counterparts during the first functional exercise and participate as the primary members' assistants. Whether they sit beside or behind depends on space available in the training room.

When the exercises become interactive, a script is used to start the sequence of events, and the team's alternate members become the Simulation Group. The starting script usually carries the exercise about 15 minutes into the allotted time. The Simulation Group then uses a menu of events to apply, as directed by the Exercise Controller, who is again guided by the rate at which the emergency management team is learning and the exercise's objectives are being achieved. Training the Simulation Group is essential; its members must understand that their role is to force integrated decision making without overstressing or understressing the emergency management team. They must also coordinate the introduction of events from the menu and manage the simulated field resources being directed by the emergency management team for realism.

After the exercise process is understood by participants (usually after two functional exercises), good results are obtained by exchanging roles. The emergency management team's primary members become the Simulation Group, and their alternates take their places in the Crisis Management Center. If the forthcoming role swap is described as the exercising process begins, the Simulation Group can usually be counted on not to overstress their primary counterparts.

Gathering data for a complete Lessons Learned List that will provide useful feedback before the next exercise requires thought beforehand and a thorough review and analysis period afterward. The lessons learned can involve changes in crisis management training *and* changes in business units' operations to avoid the disruptive event that was simulated.

A cautionary note: Participants in all exercises should accept reality. Decisions must be made with insufficient information against time deadlines that arrive much faster than decision makers would prefer. Control to achieve training objectives has to be clear and effective. If that cannot be achieved, participants may become unmotivated to participate in the ongoing process.

Tabletop exercises are a good way to familiarize participants with the emergency management system and plan, but during the functional exercises that follow tabletops, more sophisticated learning takes place. Functional exercises require a Simulation Group, whose role is to send messages that simulate developing events and then to respond to the emergency management team's direction as though they are the actual resources that the team will try to use.

In preparing simulators to focus on exercise objectives, I recommend involving about six emergency management team alternates *as a group* in creating the messages to start the exercise. They should also develop an extensive list of messages that can advance the exercise, although each and every message may not be used. During those group sessions, include discussions about their roles and their authority to improvise events when the list of messages is not achieving the objectives. They should also be briefed on why and how to suspend or stop an exercise, which is discussed later.

▶ Controlling Exercises to Maximize Learning

Although there can be but one Exercise Controller, the Controller must rely on the Simulation Group to alert him or her when the emergency management team is not coordinating its responses to developing situations. The Controller can then choose messages from the menu that are more likely to help the emergency management team learn to integrate their management, or the Controller can involve the simulators in creating an event and sending in messages to do that. Please note that the technique of management exercising does *not* involve assessing the judgment of the emergency management team. At first, members will need improvement simply because they are learning a new skill — integrated emergency management — as a group, but readers will see improvement with practice. The best practice of exercising as a technique impels the management team to learn integrated decision making under stress.

A note about stress is appropriate here. Too much stress results in frustration and slows or interrupts the learning process. Too little stress results in boredom, with the same effect. It is important to have an observer in the Crisis Management Center whose job is to report to the Exercise Controller about a member who is approaching a high frustration level and to tell the Controller about a member who appears bored. The Exercise Controller then coordinates the Simulation Group to reduce the workload of the frustrated team member or to occupy the bored one.

Involving the business units in setting objectives subordinate to the exercise's principal ones keeps the planner away from potential conflicts caused by inflexibility. During planning for exercises, the participation of representatives from those business units that will be implementing emergency plans is essential.

When it becomes apparent that one or more members of the team are not learning or that the situation has become confused, it is good practice to recall that, because the underlying purpose is learning, suspending the exercise to clarify the situation is a good thing. Should an actual major disruptive event occur, the Exercise Controller should suspend the exercise until enough information is available to decide whether the exercise's major players or enough other players will be needed to deal with the actual emergency. Of course, if the actual emergency becomes a major event, the exercise should be terminated and all resources returned to available status without delay. Those rules should be made part of pre-exercise briefings for everyone involved and should be re-iterated at the beginning of each exercise.

➤ Collecting the Lessons Learned

This section describes the review and analysis sessions. Please note that terminology. It is designed to avoid the word "critique," which implies criticism and a potential for embarrassment. By avoiding that concept, postexercise follow-up activities are more likely to facilitate positive results. After every exercise, complete lists of lessons learned should be collected from the groups involved. The manager responsible for emergency preparedness can then review the complete lists and prepare a report with recommendations for senior management.

We have now gone through Steps 1 through 8 of those necessary to build a plan and supporting program to avoid disasters.

■ STEP 9: PUBLIC RELATIONS AND CRISIS COORDINATION

Step 9 is about public relations and related communications issues. When managers realize that loss of confidence by employees and their families, investors, regulators, customers, suppliers, and the public at large is one of the more severe long-term effects of the inability to stave off a disaster and that it may, in fact, become a second disaster, there is a tendency to try to minimize damage by withholding information. Sadly, that usually exacerbates problems.[13]

To withhold information — even with the admirable intention of saying nothing until the data are complete — is simply to give others a blank canvas on which to paint the picture.

Not all those would-be painters have your company's best interests at heart.

It might be useful to begin expanding this topic by outlining today's media environment. I have had conversations on this issue with many managers while mentoring policy groups at the Emergency Management Institute and while instructing university crisis management courses.[14] Most wonder why some eyewitness or so-called expert who seems more like a candidate for institutional care can get onto a TV screen and describe how a company let some crisis happen or how it was mismanaged. Here are some facts bearing on this repeated pattern.

Of the 24 hours of TV station programming, about 20 hours are under contract (i.e., filled with network shows). That leaves station managers about four hours to do something that will beat the competition's ratings. For that, they use local news coverage. Local stations pour many millions into their news departments, and the pressure to beat the competition comes in two forms: First is the scoop: to get the story on the air before the other local stations, if even by only a minute or two. Second is the local angle: Reporters watch and listen for the *hook* — something to make viewers stop surfing and watch *their* story.

When the assignment editor tells the reporter, "Go out there and send in the story," the editor does *not* mean ". . . if the company will cooperate," but rather, ". . . or you won't be working here for long!" Reporters for radio and TV are always on deadlines. Reporters for newspapers and magazines know that "Stop the presses!" is only a line from an old movie. *All* reporters know that people in the news business get fired every day. Therefore, when an authoritative source is not quickly available, reporters will listen to *and quote* a source with even tenuous ties to the incident. Here are some countermeasures that managers with the need to do something positive, and in a hurry, can put in place as part of a disaster avoidance plan:

➤ Realize that the event has already happened. Whatever the facts are, they cannot be changed substantially.

➤ Put a system in place to get the basic facts to your spokesperson very quickly.

➤ Realize that the employee loyalty of previous years is no longer something that managers can count on. Reporters have sources inside and outside your organization. Disgruntled employees, ex-employees, and neighbors have their own agendas and will contact the media.

➤ Recognize that the media comes to you with these general mind-sets:

    ➤ Local reporters know that you are part of their community, and they will be coming to you for future stories.

    ➤ Regional reporters are usually disinterested in community angles. Their approach is like the line from a famous TV series: "Just give us the facts, please." They will work out a regional hook—usually with human-interest overtones.

    ➤ Major network personalities will develop their own hooks. Your company's spokespersons cannot change those, but they can watch for chances to use them.

With that knowledge, here are some guidelines to include in the public relations part of your company's plan:

➤ *Rule Number 1:* Never lie.

➤ *Rule Number 2:* Appoint a single spokesperson.

➤ *Rule Number 3:* The format is who, when, what, where, why, and how.

Each of those rules is followed by a "However":

➤ *However Number 1:* The spokesperson does not have to tell *everything* the company knows.

➤ *However Number 2:* When it gets big enough, the single spokesperson will have to step aside for your company's big kahuna.

➤ *However Number 3:* Before releasing personal information, clear the "who" part with HR, especially when there are casualties; and before addressing causes, clear the "why" with legal, investor relations, and the regulatory liaison, especially when there may be liability exposure or other issues that they will know about.

A note to the public relations spokesperson: Build your relationships with local and regional reporters *before* a crisis develops. If they aren't there before it hits the fan, the company will be in the soup. Get their home phones, cell phones, fax numbers, and e-mail addresses.

The essence of what follows should become part of the public relations representative's checklist for crisis use: Communicate up, communicate laterally, and communicate down. Here's what that means in plain language:

Communicate up: Don't let your bosses get an unpleasant surprise. If all you have time for is a 3 A.M. call saying, "Boss, please turn on your TV," then do that. The chairman of the board may already be watching the breaking news coverage.

Communicate laterally: Remember reporters' work environment. Get what facts you have to them as soon as you can. Don't wait until you have perfect information because no one ever will, but someone with his or her own agenda will provide so-called facts unless you are first. Keep sending information to reporters because they are your company's initial link to employees, investors, regulators, and the general public. Frequent press releases as more facts are known or even when there is nothing new to report can forestall creative writing.

Don't omit company employees. Without a doubt, they are the most vital group for your organization's future. Your spokesperson should know what they want to know before he or she looks into the cameras' lenses. The spokesperson should also realize that when speaking to the employees, the spokesperson (and especially when the big kahuna becomes your company's spokesperson) is also speaking to employees' families. Media releases should also be crafted to address investors. When investors lose confidence, a company's stock price goes into free fall. An important message is to project the image that your outfit is planned and trained to manage crises and that it is on top of developments.

Just as employees have families, regulators have bosses. Their bosses will be asking what is going on. Early in the communications process, the CMT's representative responsible for governmental liaison should send messages that arm the regulators with facts. Otherwise, be ready for new and more restrictive regulations after the crisis.

Communicate down: Before an event occurs, make sure that your company's employees know the single-spokesperson policy, and that it means the person on the CMT, not the first person in touch with a reporter. An 800 number to your message recorded for employees can really help, and using your organization's Web site with a password link to get and post situation reports will save both employee relations and human relations hours on the phone.

Also before the event strikes, business unit managers should know what information they need to get *very quickly* up to the CMT and that they should not wait for the complete set of facts that will never come. Make sure that your Emergency Response Teams in the field know that situation reports are one of their responsibilities—their essential part of communicating in a crisis.

■ STEP 10: AVOIDING DISASTER AND INTERACTION WITH GOVERNMENT AGENCIES

The tenth and final step in building a disaster avoidance program is to prepare for interaction with the governmental agencies that should also be concerned with keeping disruptive events from triggering that decline toward catastrophe. Chapter 8 is devoted to that issue, but right now is a good time to set forth some basic facts and start thinking about it.

September 11, 2001, should have made it obvious that governments have a very large stake in maintaining their communities' quality of life through their economic well-being. Some communities and regional government agencies had realized that even before September 11, and they began coordinating and cooperating with resident companies that are their communities' economic drivers. Realistically however, getting to real partnerships in emergency preparedness means overcoming the internal cultures of both most agencies and most corporations. Government agencies can help, stand by, or hinder your company's efforts to avoid disaster. Helping your company get to real partnering for emergency preparedness is what Chapter 8 is all about.

Appendix A: Crisis Management Center Supplies and Equipment

Expendable Supplies

Markers, permanent and erasable, eraser and board cleaning fluid

Emergency management forms[15]

Attendance rosters

Event logs

Major events record

Incident Briefing form (ICS 201)

Incident Objectives form (ICS 202)

Damage Assessment and Control log

Intelligence and Plans log

Logistics Requirements and Procurement log

Financial Expenditures and Planning log

Information Requests and Releases log

Legal and Regulatory Issues and Actions log

Regular forms

Purchase orders

Personnel action forms

Time sheets

Site plots

Buildings' floor plans

Maps of surrounding areas

Lined pads, pens, pencils, envelopes, tape, in-out baskets, and similar items for each management position

Phone or radio message recording and routing forms

Easels with chart pads, masking tape

Spare batteries and blank microcassette tapes

Equipment

Table sign holders

Vests identifying key functions
Manual pencil sharpener
White boards
3 freestanding display supports (easels)
Displays (displays should be covered with writable trans
  parent film and markers to match)
    Where available, a screen with projected summaries of
        Major events
        Own business units' status
    Involved building
    Involved site
    Surrounding area map
Telephone instruments to match lines pulled into Crisis
  Management Center
Chargers to match managers' cellular phones
Chargers to match the handheld radios in use on site
Radio frequency scanner programmed to mutual aid and
  public safety frequencies with list of important fre-
  quencies
Emergency lighting
    Headlamps
    Flashlights
    Light sticks
2 battery-operated clocks

Available Nearby

Computers
    Internet connections
    Proprietary LAN and WAN connections
Printer to match computers
Tape recorders, handheld
Copier
Fax machine
Calculator

Traffic direction barriers and writable directional signs
Self-contained fire extinguishers
Alternate power source with independent fuel supply
Cameras and film (including video)
Toilets
Access keys
Commercial AM-FM radio
Commercial TV

Appendix B: Representative Crisis Management Functions

Descriptions of the Duties and Relationships of the Integrated Emergency Management Structure

Manager/Director.   The Crisis Management Center manager should determine the level of response required by the situation, activate the Crisis Management Center at the appropriate stage, direct and coordinate response and restoration activities within the company, maintain liaison with senior management, authorize specific response actions for issues brought to the Crisis Management Center manager, and assign resource priorities when necessary.

Advance Planning.   The Plans and Intelligence manager should use the available information to estimate the requirements for the next planning period, outline those estimates for each of the other functional managers, confer with them to validate or modify the estimates and to receive their collectively proposed courses of action, confer with the Crisis Management Center manager to determine the interval for situation reports by the other Center functional managers, provide guidance to the other Center functional managers for advance planning, and submit the estimated requirements and proposed courses of action to the Center manager prior to decision time for the next planning period.

Alerting and Warning.   The _____ manager should pass information about hazardous situations within and outside the company and use the information to initiate any stage of Center activation.

Regulatory Liaison.   The _____ manager should establish contact with the regulatory agencies and provide

FUNCTIONS	CMC MANAGER	PLANS & INTELLIGENCE	FACILITIES & LOGISTICS	HUMAN RESOURCES	FINANCE & ADMINISTR'N	INFORMATION SERVICES	LEGAL COUNSEL	RESPONDER LIAISON	PUBLIC RELATIONS	EXECUTIVE ASSISTANT
EXEC. MANAGEMNNT	PRIMARY	SUPPORT	SUPPORT	SUPPORT	SUPPORT	SUPPORT	SUPPORT	SUPPORT	SUPPORT	
ADVANCE PLANNING		PRIMARY								
ALERTING & WARN'G		SUPPORT							SUPPORT	
CASUALTY MGT			PRIMARY	SUPPORT		SUPPORT				
LIAISON W/ REGULATORS		SUPPORT	SUPPORT	SUPPORT		SUPPORT	PRIMARY	SUPPORT	SUPPORT	
DAMAGE ASSESMT		SUPPORT	PRIMARY			SUPPORT	SUPPORT	SUPPORT	SUPPORT	
DAMAGE CONTROL	PRIMARY		PRIMARY							
DEMOBILIZATION		SUPPORT	SUPPORT	SUPPORT	SUPPORT	SUPPORT	SUPPORT	SUPPORT	SUPPORT	
DOCUMENTATION/RECS		SUPPORT	SUPPORT	SUPPORT	PRIMARY	SUPPORT	SUPPORT			
CMC ADMINISTRATION		SUPPORT	SUPPORT	SUPPORT		SUPPORT				PRIMARY
EXPENDTURE TRACK.		SUPPORT	SUPPORT		PRIMARY					
FACILITIES MGT.			PRIMARY							
FAMILY RELATIONS				PRIMARY					SUPPORT	
I.S. & TELECOMMUNS		SUPPORT	SUPPORT			PRIMARY		SUPPORT		
LEGAL ADVICE							PRIMARY	SUPPORT		
LODGING			PRIMARY	SUPPORT	SUPPORT	SUPPORT				
MATERIALS AND SUPPLY			PRIMARY	SUPPORT	SUPPORT	SUPPORT		SUPPORT		
OPER. RESTORATION		SUPPORT	SUPPORT	SUPPORT		SUPPORT		SUPPORT		
PUB&EMPLYEE INFO	SUPPORT	SUPPORT	SUPPORT	SUPPORT	SUPPORT	SUPPORT			PRIMARY	
RECOVERY PLANNING		PRIMARY	SUPPORT	SUPPORT	SUPPORT	SUPPORT	SUPPORT	SUPPORT	SUPPORT	
RESPONDERS LIAISON		SUPPORT		SUPPORT	SUPPORT	SUPPORT		PRIMARY	SUPPORT	
RELOCATION		SUPPORT	PRIMARY	SUPPORT	SUPPORT	SUPPORT			SUPPORT	
SAFETY & SECURITY		SUPPORT	PRIMARY	SUPPORT	SUPPORT	SUPPORT				
SITUATION ANALSIS	PRIMARY	SUPPORT	SUPPORT	SUPPORT	SUPPORT	SUPPORT	SUPPORT	SUPPORT	SUPPORT	
TRAFFIC CONTROL		SUPPORT	PRIMARY	SUPPORT	SUPPORT	SUPPORT				
TRANSPORTATION		SUPPORT	PRIMARY	SUPPORT	SUPPORT	SUPPORT				
VITAL RECORDS		SUPPORT	PRIMARY	SUPPORT	SUPPORT	SUPPORT	SUPPORT	SUPPORT		
LIAISON W/ INVESTORS										
LIAISON W/ CUSTOMERS										

them with initial information about the emergency including the following: origin of the event; number and severity
of casualties; physical damage to buildings, equipment, supplies, and infrastructure; estimated time that the company's
functions will be interrupted; assistance requested; and
schedule for the next contact.

Casualty Management. The _____ manager should
locate, recover, treat, and stabilize injured or ill people until assistance is available from the city's or other emergency medical services, as well as locate and safely remove
company personnel in danger or trapped. The
_____ manager may direct the company's Emergency Response Team in those activities.

Customer Liaison. The _____ manager should prioritize customers for contact and identify their information
requirements, deliver the information to them, receive feedback from them, summarize their information, notify the
Crisis Management Center manager of the feedback, and
pass appropriate information to the Crisis Management
Team.

Damage Assessment. The Facilities and Logistics manager should find, assess, and report physical damage and
other impairments to the company's ability to carry out its
mission; determine systems capability for short-term and
long-term service; estimate time and resources needed to restore the abilities; and use the Situation Reporting Form to
compile damage cost estimates.

Damage Control. The Facilities and Logistics manager
should stop damage and impairments to the organization's
ability to carry out its mission, where practical; take action
to prevent additional damage; locate, isolate, and, where
practical, stop fires and hazardous materials spills and

prevent potential fires and hazmat spills; and restrict access to unsafe areas.

Demobilization. The Crisis Management Center manager should plan an orderly and logical sequence to reduce the level of resources committed to crisis management, ensure that adequate documentation is part of the process, outline the demobilization sequence for each of the functional managers, confer with each functional manager to validate or modify the outline, and confer with the manager's staff before deciding on demobilization.

Documentation and Record Keeping. The Finance and Administration manager should collect, preserve, and secure records related to managing the emergency and other vital records that are at risk, including duplicating records and storing copies off-site. This function also has responsibilities for the Expenditures Tracking function listed later. In preparation, the Finance and Administration manager should determine the format that insurers and other potential reimbursement providers require and have master copies on hand and off-site.

Crisis Management Center Administration. The Crisis Management Center manager's assistant should screen incoming communications and pass them to the appropriate functional managers, assist the manager with situation analyses, note actions assigned to functional managers by the manager, remind functional managers and the manager of responses due when necessary, keep the major events display and log current, and anticipate and request human-factors requirements for Crisis Management Center Team members. The manager's assistant is not in the direct line of authority but has the key support role, reporting directly to the manager.

Expenditures Tracking. The Finance and Administration manager should capture and record extraordinary expenses related to the emergency in detail and in formats suitable for reimbursement and later audit by either insurance or other providers, provide cost analyses related to the emergency, facilitate planning for future emergencies, ensure that related records are accurate, and write cost-savings recommendations into After Action Reports.

Facilities Management. The Facilities and Logistics manager should set up, maintain, and demobilize incident support facilities including custodian services; provide security at organization facilities and supply food as needed for organization personnel unable to leave their assignments; monitor, protect, and restore organization facilities' infrastructure; and coordinate with the Relocation function's manager to locate and contract for lodging and other spaces needed.

Family Relations. The Human Resources manager should assure company personnel dealing with the emergency of their families' status (enabling employees to concentrate on the organization's emergency); proactively provide company employees with hazard information and self-protection instructions designed for their family members; determine communications pathways and message content before the event; obtain employees' family status and furnish employees' status to their families; and, when necessary, facilitate meeting families' basic needs (e.g., food, shelter, and medical treatment).

Information Services/Telecommunications. The Information Services manager should find, assess, and report physical damage and other impairments in the company's information and telecommunications systems (these functions match Damage Assessment and Damage Control but are specific to information services); stop damage and impairment of information systems where practical; estimate time and resources needed to restore information and telecommunications systems' capabilities; prevent or mitigate potential damage in advance of events; develop plans for using supplementary communications equipment, including distribution and maintenance; provide information services equipment and support to Crisis Management Center staff; arrange processing for the company's financial and other requirements at third-party facilities before needed; install and test communications and information systems equipment; and supervise the Crisis Management Center communications.

Legal Advice. Counsel should monitor developments in the Crisis Management Center for legal implications (especially exposures involving existing contracts and statutory obligations); review summaries and forecasts from Plans and Intelligence to gauge and mitigate impacts on the company's legal responsibilities; consider actions planned by the manager for implementation by the functional managers; advise manager's Staff and functional managers when priorities or implementation methods may have legal implications; maintain liaison with the Recovery Planning function (under Plans and Intelligence) to advise the manager on priorities and implementation of future recovery actions; and, when possible, attend preparedness meetings and assist with preplanning guidelines. The Legal Counsel is not in the direct line of authority but has the principal legal support role in the emergency management organization structure, reporting directly to the manager.

Lodging. The Facilities and Logistics manager should shelter and house both company employees who have to be relocated away from hazardous situations or facilities that become unable to support organization operations and organization employees who have to restore the company's operations away from their usual workplace.

Materials and Supplies. The Facilities and Logistics manager should identify supplies, equipment, services, and skills needed before an event occurs; preidentify a list of suppliers available 24-7 who have sufficient quantities and adequate planning to function during major emergencies; note suppliers outside the areas of potential natural disaster impacts affecting the company; and, during an event, contact and contract with suppliers preidentified with those capabilities for needed materials, services, and supplies.

Operational (Short-Term) Restoration. The Operations manager should determine emergency actions needed to restore critical services and establish the company's services restoration priorities using a tiered priority system.

Stakeholder and Employee Information. The Public Information manager should develop and release warnings, notifications, and other messages, both internal and external to the company, and coordinate the information provided with the manager responsible for Regulatory Liaison. Prior to emergencies, the Public Information manager should prepare standard information releases, including a company fact sheet, a format for reporting events that generate major emergencies and countermeasures applied to minimize their impacts, and prepare a sidebar on the company's foresight about disaster avoidance and business continuity planning.

Recovery Planning. The Plans and Intelligence manager should address long-term issues beyond operational (short-term) restoration. These include rebuilding, relocating, mitigation through changed processes or management approaches, and other strategic issues. At least one individual should be assigned to identify recovery issues as preparation or response begins.

Regulatory Liaison. The Regulatory Liaison manager should establish contact with regulatory agencies, keep them informed of the company's status and restoration actions, coordinate the information provided with the Public Information manager, advise the manager and Team on regulatory issues and exposures related to the emergency, and attend preparedness meetings and develop guidelines for preplanning. The Regulatory Liaison manager is not in the direct line of authority but has the role of advising the Team and the manager in the emergency management organization structure. The Regulatory Liaison manager reports directly to the manager.

Relocation. The Facilities and Logistics manager should develop and maintain a list of commercial real estate resources nearby, inform them that the organization will need enough space for the critical business units when a major event occurs, obtain the real estate contact's 24-7 contact number, add the names of the real estate contacts to this plan's Resources section, relocate organization personnel in danger or who are isolated due to the emergency/disaster, evacuate them to shelter areas with adequate facilities when necessary, determine available real estate that matches the needs of displaced operations, contract for space as necessary, plan transportation of essential supplies and equipment, and move displaced business functions.

Safety and Security Manager. The Safety and Security manager should develop and implement measures to ensure personnel safety, assess or anticipate hazardous and unsafe situations likely to develop in major emergencies, correct unsafe situations, and secure company property so that people are not exposed to hazards and so that property is protected from loss.

Situation Analysis. The Crisis Management Center manager should collect, analyze, and display situation information; prepare situation reports; determine the interval for situation reports from functional managers with the Plans and Intelligence manager; draft and document an Action Plan for each period; provide guidance to the Plans and Intelligence manager for advance planning including planning for demobilization; provide technical support to the other Crisis Management Center groups; and maintain a log and written copies of situation reports and requests for assistance.

Traffic Control. The Facilities and Logistics manager should direct pedestrian and vehicle traffic to avoid interference with emergency response and other emergency-related activities and to avoid exposing vehicles' occupants to hazards.

Transportation. The Facilities and Logistics manager should be ready with a list of vendors prepared to move materials, equipment, and people between the company's facilities and alternate work sites when normal transportation may be disrupted; arrange for transportation to move things from vendors to operating locations if needed; and advise the Plans and Intelligence manager about the status of commercial and public transportation, including routes, as needed.

Vital Records. The Facilities and Logistics manager should monitor damage assessments and damage control activities for indications that vital records may be involved; recommend actions to protect the vital records; collect, preserve, and secure vital records at risk; duplicate vital records when advisable to prevent their deterioration or disappearance; and recommend record recovery methods including the use of noninjurious extinguishing agents, control of water and corrosive agents, salvage methods and priorities, ways to stop records' self-destruction, dewatering, and restoring readability.

Chapter 4

The Senior Manager's Primer

A Chapter of Observations and Advice Uniquely for Senior Managers

This chapter is devoted to senior managers. For both senior managers and those who report to them while building a business continuity program, this may be the most rewarding chapter of the book. It is written knowing that there are so many pressing demands on senior managers' time that reading this (or an abstract of this chapter that a subordinate does for the boss) may be the best opportunity to learn enough about this vital topic.

Learn "enough" to do what?

Enough to understand its value to a corporation and to a manager's position. Enough to know whether a subordinate's proposal has the essential elements to make it viable, and whether there are elements that will probably make a proposal fail and thus should be removed. Enough to become an effective advocate, sponsor, and champion of a program that can save the company a lot of difficulty. And enough to assess progress as a program develops.

■ WHAT'S IN IT FOR THE SENIOR MANAGER?

First, there is awareness. Senior managers should be aware of potential threats to the company's ongoing business functions in order to avoid unpleasant surprises. Earlier in this book, the method for discovering and evaluating the danger from a nearly complete list of threats was outlined. When a proposal for a disaster avoidance program is presented, two or three scenarios of the threats that business unit managers have estimated to have the greatest impacts should be summarized. In addition to threat awareness, senior managers should be aware that disruptive events can quickly enter what pilots call a graveyard spiral. A disruptive event becomes a crisis, then spirals on down to become a disaster that threatens a brand's market share, and goes on to become a catastrophe—meaning that a brand may no longer be viable or, worse, that the corporation's survival is at stake, at least in its current form. At the time of this writing, Arthur Andersen is in just such a situation, and Union Carbide's months of misfortune, with sell-offs and downsizing, provide an earlier example.

Next is decision making. A senior manager decides whether to champion a program before the inevitable major disruptive event emerges from the ranks of waiting threats, and only senior management can commit the resources that can stave off, reverse, and perhaps even wrest profits from such an event.

To help senior managers evaluate disaster avoidance program proposals, I recommend that proposals' assessments of potential impacts should go past the dollar amounts that most business unit managers can produce. Appendix A of this chapter lists seven other types of impacts and includes explanations. Although they are harder to assess and quantify than the dollar amounts, those seven should have real meaning for senior managers, who have a more strategic view of the corporation and its situation.

Another aspect of decision making is that a senior manager is going to become the ultimate decision maker when a major disruptive event occurs. Whether or not the senior manager is designated in some formal way or is part of a pre-planned crisis management structure, the responsibility comes with the position.

Third, policies come from senior management, and policies will shape the company's crisis management program. Readers are encouraged to modify the example policy that follows to match their situation. Next, hiring the person to manage a crisis management program will ultimately be determined by the senior manager in a rational system. The content of reports to mark milestones and challenges during program development will be defined by the senior manager. And last of these definable items is the senior manager's responsibility for monitoring the program as it develops, shaping its evolution into a shield for the corporation.

There is also a list of less easily defined items that are nonetheless vital to developing the program with which a senior manager is identified. One is *the buzz*, or perceptions of one's peers and other employees as the program gets underway and hits major milestones. Another is the role of champion as defender because there will always be rivalry for a company's resources.

Perhaps the most positive concept for senior managers is the opportunity to make the company almost blast-proof by championing a program that can reduce impacts and sometimes even improve the company's position. With that comes the opportunity to advance a senior manager's career.

Reviewing that list of items for a senior manager's attention, what follows is an expansion on each.

■ EXPANDING ON THE BASIC CONCEPTS IMPORTANT TO SENIOR MANAGERS

➤ Policy

While some middle managers and direct reports to senior managers will offer policy suggestions, the responsibility rests at the Senior Management level for several good reasons. Only an executive at that level has the enterprise-wide scope and sense of timing for a global management environment that permits thoughtful policy composition. In addition, after some practice in writing policies and seeing how they get implemented, senior management executives have had opportunities to learn to make policies written clearly enough yet broadly enough to give the implementers adequate discretion to adjust to changing or unforeseen situations. This is especially important when writing policies that will be used under great stress with much less information than one would ordinarily have, as well as in the face of very short time constraints to direct people who are likely to be unfamiliar with their roles while working in an unimaginable situation—a pretty fair description of a Crisis Management Team or an Emergency Response Team.

Senior managers may wish to adapt the following policy statement to their own corporations:[1]

Background
Recent events underscore the wisdom of preparing for disruptive events, whether from natural, human, or accidental causes.

Policy and Goal
Our Board has established a policy to initiate enterprise-wide preparations to mitigate such events. The goal is to minimize losses within our organization.

Objectives

➤ Identify threats that will be both likely and intense for specific sites.

➤ Estimate the impacts on each mission-critical business unit.

➤ Evaluate the cost-effectiveness of mitigation strategies. Consider business continuity, high availability, and recovery for those units.

➤ Develop an implementation plan with these elements:

> ➤ Employee awareness and self-help training, including family preparedness.
> ➤ On-site emergency response teams.
> ➤ Response management.
> ➤ Coordination with local emergency response agencies.
> ➤ Crisis management.
> ➤ Interaction with policy-level management.
> ➤ Recovery management.

➤ Execute the implementation plan.

Responsibilities

➤ Business unit managers will develop business case proposals for the above objectives, including time, budget, and other resources required.

➤ Higher level managers will review those proposals, determine feasibility, and approve achievable programs for the business units that they oversee.

➤ Review conferences will be conducted as program milestones are reached, but not less often than quarterly.

> ➤ Program reviews' results will be reported to sen-
> ior management as the percentage of objectives
> achieved for each time period.
>
>   ➤ Quarterly progress reports will be reported
>   by senior management as the percentage of
>   objectives achieved, with under- and over-
>   achievements to the Board of Directors.
>
> Managers' performance evaluations henceforth
> will include the percentage of objectives attained
> in each time period.

I recognize that a policy statement that comprehensive probably reflects a major change for many organizations. For managers under contract, there has probably been little heretofore that made preparing to avoid or manage disasters part of their job descriptions. Therefore, incremental intro- duction of the policy may be the best course to reach that level. Almost certainly, adaptation to the corporate culture is going to be necessary. Where there are tightly written mem- oranda of understanding with employee representation groups, the legal department should be consulted for advice. None of those considerations can be allowed to override common sense, which—especially given the experiences of recent events initiated and highlighted by September 11, 2001—means that a company without a disaster avoidance program is a company taking unnecessary risk.

➤ Decision Making during Crises

As noted earlier, senior managers become the ultimate de- cision makers in crises—ready or not. Having considerable experience that a senior manager once described as evi- denced by "gray hair and scar tissue," and having the benefit of reading many after-action reports and management case histories in which senior managers shared what went right as well as what they wish they could return to and do over, I again offer advice. The advice comes in two parts.

One. When a tested crisis management system is in place with trained people, a senior executive usually needs only to monitor progress. However, intervention is recommended when existing policy is inadequate for new circumstances or when a very high-risk issue arises.

Two. When the system is being developed (read: " . . . you are doubtful"), policy guidance is warranted, and the following advice applies. It is in the form of a checklist for senior managers who will find themselves in the decision-maker's position when an actual crisis begins to emerge and who will want to get some management aids in place as a disaster avoidance program is being developed.

Two and a half. Be sure that subordinates know you do not mind being alerted about a crisis early on; then being informed it has been taken care of. They should also know that if you hear about it after things have gone "off the rails" or if you are called by a colleague and hear, "Turn on your TV!" you will not be the only one who is unhappy.[2]

> If an event with a senior manager involved hits before a crisis management plan and trained team are in place, please refer to Appendix B of this chapter.

When Managing a Crisis, Prioritize!

1. Establish reliable communications.

   ➤ Without good information, good decisions could rely on luck.

   ➤ Commercial television shots are not chosen to give decision makers representative or comprehensive information.

➤ Require your Emergency Response Teams to make situation reports.

➤ Get someone you know and trust at the scene with company identification and authority to keep information flowing to you.

2. Determine what you do and do not know.

➤ Have a template for essential information.

➤ Use two-way communications to obtain missing information.

➤ Get managerial help beside you as an ad hoc Crisis Management Team, and get clerical help trained to support those managers.

➤ Divide the work in this checklist by categories and assign it among the managers you bring in.

➤ Assign and train a person to monitor media statements.

3. Limit the impacts—you will be interrogated about this later.

➤ Human impacts come first.

➤ Get people out of harm's way.

➤ Get medical attention for casualties.

➤ When the event generates a threat that is (or appears to be) yours, initiate warnings to those who will be impacted.

➤ Emphasize these priorities to your ad hoc Crisis Management Team.

➤ Alert them to watch for issues that need to be bucked up to the policy level:

   ➤ When existing policy is inadequate for new circumstances.

➤ When a very high-risk issue arises.

4. Isolate the crisis to limit the impact on ongoing business operations.

➤ Advise employees not involved as your ad hoc Crisis Management Team to leave them alone, that you will keep updating internal communications (see Number 6).

➤ Make it clear that your Crisis Management Team has full authority to bring in individuals with needed expertise and that response should be without delay.

5. Determine and meet the media's needs.

➤ They must report what they see and what they can discover — or they will get fired.

➤ Do not tempt them to fill in the blanks by going to less accurate sources:

➤ Unhappy ex-employees.

➤ Single-interest groups with their own agendas.

➤ Unknowledgeable individuals seeking attention.

➤ Use the media to channel your messages to

➤ Employees.

➤ Their families.

➤ Investors.

➤ Regulators.

➤ Customers.

➤ Suppliers.

➤ The general public.

➤ Back up messages sent via the media (see Number 6).

6. Make communications easy.

➤ Collect and disseminate valid information.

➤ Use an 800 number for employees to take loads off your call center operators.

➤ Your Web site can have a password to an interactive employees' area.

➤ Keep the information current.

➤ Identify recovery issues.

➤ Support your on-scene manager's business restoration efforts.

➤ Think strategically and be proactive at the Crisis Management Team level; the on-scene manager must deal with immediate problems.

A *Crisis Brings Both Danger and Opportunity*

➤ Don't stay in the defensive mode.

➤ Think about your competitor's viewpoint.

➤ Senior executives, especially, should consider the event in a strategic light

➤ Comprehensively, and

➤ Projected over an extended time frame.

Review your company's strategic plans. Opportunity may have arrived early.

➤ Hiring

The previous lists of priorities and required information items, coupled with the beginning illustrations of why senior managers should be intensely interested in avoiding disasters, should convince the great majority of senior executives that hiring someone to oversee development of a business continuity program is a good idea. Not just anyone—but someone competent and motivated to support the executive championing this effort by pushing the program and integrating the detail work.

One way to eliminate a lot of preliminary hiring effort is to specify professional certifications. Two are designed for corporate business continuity programs. First is the Business Continuity Institute's Member and Fellow levels, with Fellow being senior, designated by the initials MBCI or FBCI after the person's name. Fellows usually come from the ranks of Members, must have years of experience, deliver examples of their work for review, pass an examination that resembles a thesis defense, and are elected a Fellow by their peers. The other certification is the Disaster Recovery Institute International's Certified Business Continuity Professional (CBCP) or Master Business Continuity Professional (MBCP). Examinations and experience are also required. Both certifications require ongoing professional updating and membership maintenance. University programs also grant degrees in the field. Some are oriented toward business, whereas many others contemplate graduates going into government jobs. The University of California at Berkeley Extension's Continuing Education in Business and Management Division certified approximately 100 through 2001, making them rare but extremely well grounded. Almost all are now corporate career professionals in business continuity.

Beyond having one of the certifications oriented toward the business world, applicants should demonstrate realization that an enterprise-wide approach is needed. Many of the early entrants into the profession came from information technology (IT) or information security careers, and some still think almost exclusively within those limits. Others came from public safety response agencies, which may give some candidates understanding of the vertical connections and of how the public and private sectors can work for mutual benefit.

Interviewers should be given instructions to probe candidates to see if their experience has provided them an outlook with that kind of breadth and depth.

Beyond hiring, senior managers are charged with selecting reporting categories and items to assure themselves that a program is on track and to become alerted should something unexpected develop.

➤ Championing Your Business Continuity Program: Progress Reports

Initially, there are reports. A senior manager and the program manager should decide together which reports are meaningful and which exceptions are cause for alarm. Depending on the corporate culture, time and budget are often given the greatest weight. I have some thoughts on whether those are meaningful. Time is of the essence because one or more of the threats identified by the business units' managers as having high impact potential will surely materialize sooner than you will want them to. The focus on time can lead to a problem.

Setting Milestones

The problem can be that someone or some group becomes apprehensive that a disruptive event will arrive before the plan matures, and therefore pressures to rush through steps that require careful thought then prove irresistible. For example, in a bank for which I once consulted, the trust department's representative assured us that the trust department need not be included among the critical business units; therefore, there was no need for early planning. Shortly thereafter, a story circulated about the trust instrument that had to be executed right after the First Interstate Bank fire,[3] and we realized that trust departments did indeed have to be included early in the planning process. For the best of reasons—trying to accelerate planning to avoid disaster—we had nearly set the bank up for a multimillion dollar loss. I point out unintended consequences—the result of bad (often hurried) decision making—several more times before this book ends. For now, it is enough to advise senior executives against sacrificing effectiveness by being pushed into arbitrary time targets.

There is another consideration in allowing time between major milestones. A very important part of developing plans is to allow the management teams to test them. This is especially true of the Crisis Management Team, which is directly connected to a representative of senior management—perhaps the executive who is reading these words. Plan testing is normally conducted during management-team training exercises. The problem that can arise is that exercise participants need time to absorb and digest the lessons that they learned during an exercise. Putting the next exercise too close to the end of the previous one is likely to interfere with that learning process, and team members will thus miss the opportunity to incorporate their inputs for improvements before the next testing and training period.

A more obvious problem is that preparations for exercises require time, effort, and financial budgeting. Put them too close together, and the managers who are preparing will burn resources that should be devoted to operating the company's principal business functions. So much for not becoming overwhelmed by overly tight time targets, except that pacing the program will help keep it within the financial budget.

Corporate Culture and Team Selection

The senior manager who champions a disaster avoidance program also makes many of the most significant inputs as the program develops, shaping it to match the corporate culture. One example is picking the managers who will become the Crisis Management Team. Although some recommendations for selecting members were made earlier, they related to observation during training exercises, so a senior executive who has had opportunities to watch candidates develop as managers and who therefore knows their strengths can save time and effort.

➤ Enterprise-Wide Emphasis

As the program develops, there are some things to watch out for. One of the most common mistakes is putting the overriding responsibility for plan development in the information systems (IS) department. Although it is true that early disaster recovery plans evolved from system crashes, the issues are now enterprise-wide and require input from several other mission-critical business units as the plan develops. As an example of why putting the overriding responsibility on the IS department can lead to unbalanced business continuity planning, one IS director was given the sole responsibility for planning, which included determining which business units were mission critical. Acting in good faith was not enough, and several business units had to resort to manual processing because their applications were not high on the priority restoration list after system crashes. It was months before senior management understood the situation and directed a change to a more comprehensive approach, which made a CBCP responsible to a senior vice president. In the meantime, morale and the productivity used to measure incentive awards in the impacted business units had tanked, creating an employee retention problem[4] to accompany the overtime costs.

Assistance during Crises

Another thing to watch for is placing an assistant to the senior management representative in the line of authority that goes above the Crisis Management Team. If you look at the organization chart for that team (see Figure 4.1), the team's manager either is, or reports directly to, a senior manager. If the proposed organization chart does not include assistants for both, the value of having them will surface with any realistic training exercise. Better to put assistants in place before that; an actual event might happen first.

Ensuring that Critical Decisions Reach the Right Level

There are situations in which a decision should be sent up from the Crisis Management Team to the senior management representative. Examples include the following:

➤ The functional managers *and* the team manager cannot select a course of action (usually when several choices are viable).

➤ Existing policy does not cover the situation.

➤ A dangerous situation (usually with potential impacts to a brand's or the company's reputation) arises.[5]

Senior managers should make sure that the Crisis Management Team manager has been instructed to bring those to you. There is, however, a however: When that becomes habitual, senior management is becoming the victim of reverse delegation. Watch out for that trend during training exercises. Also, resist the temptation to jump in before the Crisis Management Team yells for help, thus inadvertently encouraging reverse delegation.

➤ Vertical Connectivity

In our academic research papers, my collaborator, Isabel Martinez Torre-Enciso,[6] and I have postulated three levels at which disaster avoidance plans must function: policy,

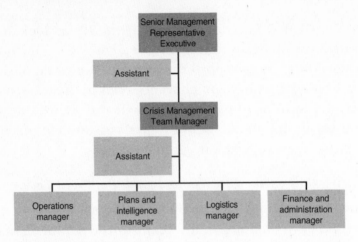

Figure 4.1 Basic Crisis Management Team organization, modified to provide assistants for the principal decision makers

middle management, and the operational level. Senior managers should review planning to satisfy themselves that the connections between those layers are in place and at first *will be*, and then later *are being*, tested successfully during training exercises.

➤ Readable and Understandable

Professionals communicate in the terminologies that ensure clarity among their colleagues—which often renders their writing incomprehensible to people in other professions. Business continuity professionals are no different; therefore, senior managers to whom business continuity professionals report should be on the lookout for the introduction of such professional jargon into plans that everyone in the company should be able to understand. I would apologize for colleagues who insist that the implementers should learn our terminology. That simply slows down progress.

■ THE SENIOR MANAGER AS CHAMPION

One way people rise to the ranks of senior management is sensitivity to a program's acceptance—or lack of acceptance. The senior managers who champion a disaster avoidance program should pay attention to reactions to their program and use them to boost or modify the program, thus making the process more efficient. No doubt others in the ranks of Senior Management will think that their own programs are worthy but impacted by a disaster avoidance program—and if that's so, make the case that the objective is to make the company blast-proof, which is good for all. When the inevitable "real-thing" test arrives, and during the exercises that provide realistic testing in the meantime, the champion's career should receive additional positive momentum. And then, when reading today's headlines or glancing at television news, there's confidence that your organization is ready.

Appendix A: Impact Types, with Examples

Human Factors Impacts

This includes all predictable effects on people following disasters and major emergencies. Obvious examples include injuries and illnesses. Less obvious examples are the near-term inability to function due to psychological decompensation, concerns about family, and the inability to communicate severe personal impacts unknown to coworkers. Latent examples include survivor guilt and posttraumatic stress disorder (PTSD). All have the potential to reduce the efficiency of an organization.

Environmental Impacts

This category consists of impacts caused by the release of things that interrupt normal ecology, including processes on which humans normally depend directly, such as breathing. The releases do not always involve the obvious ones such as hazardous materials. Milk and wine, moved in tankers, are toxic to fish. Much of the fish we eat now comes from fish farms, making the people involved in aquaculture stakeholders.

Damaged Image or Public Confidence

This category relates to diminished trust and lost certainty that an organization knows what it is doing and that its management will do the right thing. Crises can spotlight required changes that might go unnoticed from outside. Exxon comes to mind, but Union Carbide is an organization where change was imposed. On the other hand, Johnson & Johnson/McNeil and First Interstate exemplify highly positive outcomes. Groups that will be closely attentive include product end-users (the public) and government regulatory agencies, product retailers and their suppliers, employees and their families, and predatory firms specializing in hostile corporate takeovers.

Political Consequences

Elected officials are drawn to TV camera lights and reporters' microphones. When the issues are constituent safety or environmental impacts, they *must* become involved. Elected officials, like celebrities, need time on camera and to be quoted by the media. In those ways, they demonstrate that they, too, are responsive and concerned. Technology now permits this to be done from a distance. No longer is it an unvarying rule that "the first helicopter will be commandeered by a senior politician." Instead, you may hear him or her commenting from the capitol on *The News Hour*. Later, he or she is likely to hold hearings and sponsor more restrictive legislation. Where cameras repeatedly go, high-visibility surrogates often arrive. Crisis = danger + opportunity. The danger: to ignore or slight any of these solicits an additional crisis. The opportunity: Elected officials at the scene are approachable, and they control government budgeting.

Functional Impairments

This category consists of the reduced capacity to perform essential functions. Liquid oxygen (LOX) tanks that are ruptured in earthquakes (high winds, vehicle collisions) stop essential processes. Road or communications outages can prevent key people from performing critical functions. Process control is obvious. What's not so obvious is that senior managers' decision making can also be disrupted.

Legal Consequences

Formerly limited to concerns of potential liability exposures, and therefore mainly a concern for private sector management, erosion of governmental immunities and inclusion of individual managers in statutes authorizing criminal sanctions have reduced immunities while increasing risks of criminal sentencing. In addition, more governmental entities *and* corporations are now including language requiring business continuity or disaster recovery planning in their contracts with suppliers. The absence of *effective* plans may be considered a breach of contract. In addition, the failure to plan conscientiously or to add such clauses to contracts may be considered lack of due diligence by investors.

Physical Damage and Destruction

Damaged or destroyed facilities, supplies, and equipment often cause reduced functional capabilities, meaning lost production. One example is damaged magnetic disks; they are inexpensive to replace and are often insured, but the data they carry may be critical—and irreplaceable. A lost communications link controlling a process may let a minor emergency escalate to a disaster. Simpler to consider are destroyed buildings or damaged machines, but damaged buildings usually have to be rebuilt to new codes.

Appendix B: Crisis Checklist When Senior Management Is Involved

The following checklist establishes guidelines to be used when senior management executives become involved in any incident that has the potential to reflect on the organization or disrupt its operations. Examples are hostage situations, sudden death or disability, missing persons, missing aircraft, hotel fires, building collapses, and so on.

1.0 *Isolate Incident.*
    1.1 Assign Incident Management Team.
        Senior executive in charge.
        Public Information Manager—authority to requisition resources, including outside experts, as needed
        Human Resources Representative.
        Security Manager.
        Telecommunications Representative.
        Executive Assistant—authority to requisition resources as above.
        Families and friends from organization: brief, get cellular number, and dispatch to spouse/executive's home with security person (next item).
        Security in civilian suit to accompany family friend; authority to requisition resources as above; brief to make joint decisions with family friend (above).
    1.2 Sequester Incident Management Team in Incident Management Center.
        1.2.1 Center Logistics.
            Communications—responsibility: Telecommunications Representative.
            Situation displays—responsibility: Executive Assistant (coordinate with Telecomm Rep).

Center supplies and equipment—responsibility: Executive Assistant.

Refreshments—responsibility: Executive Assistant.

Security—responsibility: Security Representative.

Lodging—responsibility: Human Resources Representative.

1.2.2 Inform Remainder of Organization.

Wait until family friend is in place and has family gathered.

Notify all employees—responsibility: Public Information Manager (coordinate with Senior Executive in Charge; establish that others are not to distract Incident Management Team members)

2.0 *Stabilize Situations at Senior Management Homes.*

2.1 Establish Liaison with Family at Home *by Direct Contact.*

Family friend: Explain type of incident.

Give what information is known.

Express organization's sympathies and complete support.

Consider media attention anticipated.

Recommend bringing children in; special attention to school liaison.

Ask about executive's siblings, parents, etc.

Recommend low-profile security presence.

Consider medical condition? Discuss contacting physician with spouse.

Consider religious affiliation? Discuss contacting clergy with spouse.

Consider special friend? Discuss contacting with spouse.

Security Representative, as directed by Family Friend: Concurrence of spouse.

Obtain list of admits and do not admits.

Contact Telecomm Rep in Incident Management Center and establish secure link.

Discuss screening telephone calls and visitors (concerns: media, lawyers' reps, disturbed persons)

3.0 *Manage Incident.*

3.1 Brief Incident Management Center Team.

Establish line of authority:

Identify Senior Executive in Charge.

Establish his/her appointment by CEO/ Chair of Board.

Introduce: Public Information Manager.

Security Manager.

Human Resources Representative.

Telecommunications Representative.

Executive Assistant.

Establish that team is to discontinue routine work and devote 100% of effort to the following tasks.

Establish organization's goal: Restore stability.

Establish team's mission: Support family and organization through the duration of the incident by maintaining stability.

Establish that team may requisition resources as necessary, including expertise within the organization. Resources from outside the organization may be requisitioned when approved by Senior Executive in Charge.

Establish that all information obtained by Team is confidential until released to public. Responsibility — Public Information Manager: Keep Team informed about what has and has not yet been released.

Team responsibility: Identify stakeholder groups to be informed. Candidates: family, employees, Board, stockholders, suppliers, customers, critical incident stress management, etc.

Incident dependent: Treasurer/Controller; foreign/regional branches.

Team responsibility: Identify potential organizational resources that may be required, alert them to keep Team informed of location and means of contact, including after working hours. Determine if travel is contemplated.

Team responsibility: Recognize that these incidents usually go on for an extended time. Identify own reliefs. Notify own families of potential disruption of routines. Notify own department of high priority activities requiring diversion or delay.

Chapter 5

Good Work! Tell Everyone!

A Chapter about Communicating

This chapter is in seven parts. All seven are about different, but linked, aspects of communicating to support your disaster avoidance program. Mostly, the chapter is about *managing* communications for maximum support to your program, although some technological aspects will necessarily be addressed. The seven parts are (1) announcing the program, (2) getting valuable information to employees, (3) recruiting teams, (4) marking progress, (5) linking with outside organizations, (6) conducting information during disruptive events, and (7) After Action Reports.

■ ANNOUNCING THE PROGRAM

In general, the key to successfully conducting information to others is to understand the needs and mindsets of the person or group with whom you are trying to communicate, as well as the needs and attitudes of the media through whom you want to communicate.[1] First, let us focus on telling people in your company.

Most employees will welcome the news that your company is undertaking a disaster avoidance program. At the

operational level, many will have been exposed to the term
emergency management, which is the term that U.S. government agencies use for all phases and that I use to describe
support for a company's Emergency Response Teams. Whatever term you use, many employees will be thinking that a
program has already been in place, so you may want to emphasize that this new program is an improvement.

■ GETTING VALUABLE INFORMATION TO EMPLOYEES

Employees' interests include preserving their jobs, keeping
their company competitive, preserving the value of their
shares and stock options, being provided with personal safety
information (especially where high-intensity natural disasters occur, e.g., flooding, hurricanes, earthquakes, and tornados), and being provided with safety information that they
can take to their families. Although employees seldom think
about it *before* a disruptive event, they will need to know how
to get basic information from their employer: Should I come
in? Now? To my usual workplace? Therefore, employees will be
glad to hear that the program will address those issues and provide a source for quickly getting comprehensive information
to them in a major disruptive event. After knowing your employees' needs comes knowing about conduits for that information. When thinking about ways to communicate with
employees *during* crises, there are several conduits to consider.

Alerting Systems

In-house e-mail is a natural extension of the now-typical
conduit for routine communications. Internet e-mail is also
very useful for two-way communications with traveling executives. Telephones become important when e-mail is not
effective or when it is important to know instantly whether

your message has been delivered—or understood. Pagers work like telephones in that regard, and two-way pagers allow reassurance that a message has been received. Regarding telephones, one of the simplest ways of getting a message to a lot of people in a reasonable time is the long-established and low-tech telephone tree, or cascade system. One person calls two people, each of whom call two more, and so on. It has a few drawbacks, notably that the phone number database (which must be continuously updated) has to be known to many participants, that some people will be reluctant to have their 24-7 phone numbers known to others in the tree, and that one cascade's tributary will stop when it reaches a member who does not call two more.

Automated Alerting

There are several technological improvements on the manpower-intensive calling tree for telephones and pagers. Depending on the number of telephone lines connected, a calling system can deliver hundreds or thousands of calls with a message in a few minutes. The more sophisticated ones can determine whether the call was answered, as well as whether by a human or a machine. Those are typically used to alert Crisis Management Team members when a disruptive event mandates their presence in the company's Crisis Management Center. They can also be used after an event to advise other employees whether, when, and where to report for work, although a simpler way is to couple standing instructions for all employees to call an 800 number with a recorded announcement. Of course, using a single telephone provider presupposes that its system is likely to remain functional. Putting all the eggs in one basket, especially for emergency communications, is seldom a good idea. In that regard, peace of mind can be cheaply obtained. A better way is to ensure that the company can access more than one phone service provider; the same caveat applies to using Internet services for employee communications.

Using commercial broadcasts or government-controlled alerting systems (i.e., community-licensed cable TV crawlers) to contact a company's employees during a major emergency remains more a theoretical concept than an effective practice to date.

Tying Employees and Families to Disaster Avoidance

An opportunity for positive contacts with employees comes with one of the early steps forward in disaster avoidance: employee self-protection. An important capability in avoiding disasters is giving every employee guidelines on what to do to minimize exposure to personal harm. That should be done before disruptive events occur. As examples, in earthquake and tornado country, employees receive guidance to get away from windows and to get under something substantial; where flooding occurs, they are told not to drive across areas where they cannot see the roadway, and so forth. Among others, the American Red Cross produces pamphlets for this kind of awareness at nominal cost.[2] Distributing them as part of your company's disaster avoidance program is an example of combining messages for employees' benefit.

One of the lessons learned from September 11, 2001, was that employees' families should be included in the information made available before disruptive events occur. At minimum, they should receive self-protection guidelines and information about how to contact the company for news of their relatives.[3]

■ RECRUITING TEAMS

Another opportunity to communicate with employees while advancing your disaster avoidance program occurs while recruiting Emergency Response Team members. One way to reduce the cost and accelerate the process of getting that pilot Emergency Response Team in place is to recruit people who are already predisposed enough to have previously obtained the training. Circulating the survey in Appendix A of this chapter can induce a positive awareness among employees who may wonder how the program will take shape at their level.

■ PROGRESS REPORTS

Progress reports marking major program milestones should be used to advantage. A progress report can be rewritten as an internal or public information release to keep your disaster avoidance program in the minds of employees and other stakeholders and to demonstrate that the program is moving forward.

■ LINKING WITH OUTSIDE ORGANIZATIONS

➤ Linking Your Disaster Avoidance Program

Linking with outside organizations is an aspect of communicating that is too often overlooked. When conducting training, it will become apparent that outside resources needed only during emergencies must be quickly available. It follows that making contact with those resources' vendors in advance is logical. What is often overlooked is the need to be able to contact them outside of normal working hours, and not just with some representative of the vendor, but with someone who has authority to say yes to urgent requests, perhaps for large quantities and to unusual delivery points. Do not forget to ask whom to contact, and how, when the primary person is not available. Confirm the contacts' names and telephone numbers at least twice each year. Making those confirmations part of preparations for management training exercises is logical and is an effective use of time. A more efficient alternative may be assigning the task of maintaining the resource database to a summer intern or other temporary assistant.

Companies without their own predisaster planning may have trouble understanding your need for that information, or even understanding what you are requesting. As an example, I had two very different responses from banks where another financial institution made overnight deposits while establishing those links for a client. One bank's representative immediately responded with the name and a 24-7 phone number for an alternate contact several states away in the event that the local contact person was out of touch because of a regional disaster. The other bank's representative honestly thought our request was some kind of joke—nowhere near April Fools' Day.

There are numerous examples of resources seldom considered until a major disruptive event arises: critical incident stress debriefers, local police liaison capabilities, kidnap and hostage consultants, large mobile electrical power generators, mobile steam generators (for some buildings and climates), and more. No matter how well thought-out a resource vendor's list is, it is unlikely to meet your needs without the advance communication that assures 24-7 contacts with the right person.

No other example of the benefits from advance contacts quite matches communications with the media, where the need for the rapport that comes from maintaining communications between disruptive events becomes obvious in a crisis. The tragic poisonings by cyanide inserted into nationally marketed nonprescription pain medication capsules provides an excellent illustration of the benefits derived from maintaining good advance communication when that most unexpected event occurred.

Both the media's reporters and the company's investigators wanted to know if there was any way that the cyanide might have gotten into the capsules during production. The company's initial investigations found none, and its press releases said so. However, several days into the event, a reporter learned that there was cyanide at one of the manufacturing sites. That reporter called the manufacturer's public relations executive, saying that he had been told cyanide was present at that site. The executive asked him not to publish that information until the company had time to get more facts. Could the cyanide contact the production runs? Had there been enough on the premises to account for five deaths? Did shipments from that plant go to the Chicago area, where the deaths had occurred? The rapport and trust built over previous years held, and the reporter agreed to hold the story. But, of course, nothing stays confidential indefinitely.

When a second reporter called the executive, enough facts had been learned that it was clear that the cyanide was only in a testing lab and was almost certainly not the cause of the deaths. By then he knew: The cyanide was kept in a separate building; very little was ever on the premises; none of it was missing; and it could not have gotten into the product. The executive released the first reporter from his pledge and provided the media with the facts from the company's investigation. The result was that information became part of follow-on stories on inside pages of most newspapers, and their reports did not suggest that an incriminating discovery had been made.[4]

Insurers are another category for communications attention while developing a disaster avoidance program. When the risk assessment scenarios are given to mission-critical business unit managers for their impact estimates, the company's insurers should be contacted to determine whether their coverage includes the likely losses in the high-impact scenarios. Precise communication during program development about what is and what is not covered, as well as about when and how claims will be paid can save millions of dollars—and perhaps the company—when severe losses accompany a major disruptive event. Disaster avoidance program managers should stay alert for changes brought on by the insurer's experience. Since September 11 insurance against terrorist acts has become both scarce and expensive,[5] to no one's surprise. However, it is possible to be surprised by loss information that insurers receive about disasters that receive little notice in the popular media but cause adverse rate and coverage changes. Most of those changes take effect at policy renewal time, of course, but advance warning before the budget cycle begins is an advantage.

► Communicating with First Responders and Public Safety

A final recommendation about communicating your company's disaster avoidance planning: Public safety agencies will respond to almost every event that has physical damage or personnel casualties. To be of greatest help, their officers-in-charge (more frequently called incident commanders or ICs) will need site and building diagrams, familiarity with your company's Emergency Operations Center, predefined communications pathways, and acquaintance with the manager supporting your Emergency Response Teams. Involving the local emergency responders in your company's Emergency Response Team training, especially exercises, can be very helpful when major disruptive events occur later. Chapter 8 contains more about the relationship between company and local government agencies.

➤ **Communicating with Internal
and External Auditors**

"Communicating" might be too strong an analogy. The concept here is simply that auditors can be the disaster avoidance program manager's friend . . . and his or her boss's friend. Here is an outside organization, probably representing your company's insurers or investors, who want reassurance that the program is in place and effective. Using the standards outlined in Chapter 9, they can make a good case that your program is working well — or they can help draw attention to your need for help. Where the internal auditors become involved, so much the better.

■ CONDUCTING INFORMATION DURING DISRUPTIVE EVENTS

➤ **Getting Facts Quickly**

This section begins with management's basic information requirements and then addresses the external aspects.

Emergency Response Teams were discussed earlier in this book, and a proposed training curriculum was provided. Team leaders should understand that one of their duties is to move basic information about casualties, damage, and lost operating capabilities on up the line of authority. True enough, but a team leader who is simultaneously trying to evacuate casualties, stop a fire from extending, and shut down a process likely to produce a hazardous material spill is not going to get off a report very quickly, except perhaps something like "Help!" Alternate reporting methods are necessary.

One method of obtaining information is to send a manager with no other duties and a reputation for keeping his or her cool to the scene with more than one way to communicate to the Crisis Management Team. Of course, the candidate for this task needs fair warning that the task will be coming his or her way. If your program includes those individuals (who may be looking at a scene on another continent) in training exercises, most potential difficulties will be foreseen, resulting in adequate information sooner. In an attempt to match advice given to senior managers in the previous chapter,[6] Figure 5.1 presents a matrix of basic facts needed that can be printed on a pocket card.

Because you cannot get more than a few words on a pocket card, the guidelines that go with it during distribution of its first draft for your company should mention writing on the card's back or keeping something else to write on close at hand. The real point is that if the responsible managers at both ends of the communication pathway have something like that tool, the basic facts about the crisis are more likely to be in hand sooner, and better decisions become possible sooner. Keep copies in your desk, on hand while commuting, and in your nightstand and your desk at home. And what if I have not thought of everything, or something more is needed for specific management environments? Here again, use the model during management training exercises, and the users will tell you any required modifications when they hand in their Lessons Learned Lists.

➤ Using the Data for Decision Making

After the initial information is in hand and updates are scheduled, the primary communications task becomes distributing the information among the Crisis Management Team members for decision making, then beyond the team for information to other stakeholders and alerts to senior management for specific situations. Distribution among the Crisis Management Team is relatively easy if the functional titles (Operations, Plans, etc. are associated with the

NATURE OF EVENT _____
   Time began: _____
LIFE SAFETY
   Known casualties: dead _____
                        injured _____
                        missing _____
   Location(s):
   Potential life hazard?
EXTENSION
   Can this event go off premises?
   If not, will others think it can?
OPERATIONAL CAPABILITIES LOST

_____

DAMAGE:

_____

ENVIRONMENTAL DAMAGE
   Known:
   Potential?
ACTIONS TAKEN

_____

ACTIONS PLANNED

_____

SITUATION FORECAST

_____

REQUESTS

_____

RECOMMENDATIONS

_____

ANTICIPATED DURATION

_____

Figure 5.1   Format to capture basic information from the initial report (pocket card)

emergency management functions listed in the grid in Appendix B to Chapter 3. The distribution task most logically falls to the Crisis Management Team's manager and his or her assistant. After the incoming information is given to the team's functional managers, it is their responsibility to develop integrated resolutions and coordinate their response. The Crisis Management Team manager and assistant remain involved by keeping the process within reasonable time limits until answers emerge from the team.

The next issue is which information should be sent internally to senior management. There are two kinds: (1) issues that cannot be resolved given the policy and other guidance in hand, and (2) issues that are dangerous to the ongoing business of the company, including items that endanger the company's reputation. This takes us to a term that some readers will have heard and that may be new to others: *reputation management.*

Three reputations notably at stake are the company's, the decision makers', and the disaster avoidance program's—which is inextricably linked to that program's manager. No doubt more than a few readers are mentally listing several others, which is expected and welcome. My principal point is that covering information management policy with an eye to those three will keep others in favorable regard, too. The company's reputation has a lot to do with its ability to attract investors, good managers to become employees, nonexcessive oversight by regulators, and—of increasing importance in the contemporary business environment—leading researchers, engineers, and desirable partners for potential mergers. It is important to note that adept management that avoids disaster can enhance the company's reputation—and the reverse can push a disruptive event toward a graveyard spiral.

Decision makers' reputations are determined largely after the event by the outcomes. If for no other reason, senior managers and policy-level executives should take a personal interest in their companies' disaster avoidance programs and should participate in rehearsals (more often called management training exercises). Those should include reviewing the media policy for disruptive events and simulations of speaking to their stakeholders through the media. Such practices increase executives' comfort levels and markedly enhance performance.

Perhaps the most notable example since the September 11 terrorist attacks is that of U.S. Secretary of Defense Donald Rumsfeld's frequent appearances before the Pentagon press corps. His unwavering lock on the messages to be delivered, apparent absorption of prebriefing supporting data, and relaxed delivery—to the point of seeming to enjoy the process—offer compelling evidence that very senior policy makers can enhance their reputations in crises.

➤ External Releases

As to the third aspect of reputation—that of managing outgoing information—please see the example in Appendix B of this chapter. Readers are urged to make adaptations to fit their corporate cultures and companies' circumstances; a multinational corporation may find several modifications appropriate to the cultures in which it conducts business.

A note of explanation is appropriate here. Introducing the term *reputation management* is not meant to indicate that crisis management is becoming mainly reputation management, as some writers have postulated.[7] However, a diminished reputation is one of the potential impacts that a well thought-out disaster avoidance program should be structured to minimize, and Crisis Management Teams should include that element of disaster avoidance in their training, to enhance their company's reputation.

➤ Internal Releases

One of the reasons for having a Crisis Management Team is to isolate a disruptive event, permitting the rest of the company to get on with its principal productive mission. The policy that establishes that arrangement should include instructions that the rest of the company is to leave the Crisis Management Team alone unless called on to provide expertise. If that is going to work for long, the tradeoff is to satisfy the natural curiosity of the team's fellow employees by providing frequent and accurate updates.

Overlooking that element of the structure invites morale problems caused by lack of information at minimum, and more often rumors—most of which are adverse and are caused by someone's yielding to the temptation to show off by saying more than he or she knows.[8] The principle here is that silence gives rumor initiators' overactive imaginations and hostile groups a blank canvas. Appendix C of this chapter presents a series of steps to keep accurate and timely information flowing to employees not directly involved in the Crisis Management Team. Readers are urged to modify these steps to meet the needs of their corporate cultures and the specific site's cultural environment.

■ AFTER ACTION REPORTS

A requirement for government organizations following each major disruptive event is an After Action Report. Its purpose is to provide a record of what occurred, what parts of the preparations and training were helpful, and what parts can be improved.

I strongly recommend that companies also prepare After Action Reports, parts of which can be designated as company confidential or otherwise assigned limited distribution. Aside from a record for the corporation's historical archive, After Action Reports are valuable as factual records for use by a company's attorneys in defense against allegations of inadequate preparations for foreseeable events or allegations that information received in time for use to mitigate losses was ignored. The principle is that a rationally planned (not "optimal"—no one has achieved that yet) and conscientiously trained team's effort easily passes what legal professionals refer to as the "reasonable person test." In other words, given the training, resources, and information at hand, a reasonable person would likely have done what was done and avoided doing what was not done.

Another potential use is for executives who may be accused of lack of due diligence by a stockholder or other stakeholders. A corollary to the previous principle is that the absence of such a record gives the opposition a blank canvas on which to paint a representation of their own agenda.

Perhaps the best application of After Action Reports is their use by the disaster avoidance program manager to make logical improvements to the program's plans, training, and other preparations before the next time one of the threats becomes reality. After Action Reports are the equivalent following actual events of the Lessons Learned Lists collected after management training exercises. When circulated among parts of the corporation that did not experience the same event, they can be used to spare them the gray hair and scar tissue that comes from grueling experience, while providing them the information necessary to improve their own readiness.

In formatting After Action Reports, much the same information that is useful in initial reports of a major disruptive event can be used, with the addition of some information that would not be available in early reports:

➤ Executive summary

➤ Nature of the event

➤ Day, date, and time it began

➤ Communications employed and their effectiveness

➤ Number of dead, injured, and missing

➤ Location of casualties

➤ Nature and severity of their injuries

➤ Effects of company Emergency Response Teams

➤ Effectiveness of Team's training, supplies, and equipment

➤ Extension of the event's effects

➤ Impacts on business operations

➤ Comparison of the impacts to preplanning scenarios

➤ Extent to which preplanning restored operations, and comparison to estimated restoration times

➤ Physical damage

➤ Extent to which insurance or other reimbursements covered losses

➤ Impacts of financial preplanning

➤ Cash flow, revenue, and profits changes

➤ Environmental damage

➤ Extent to which reporting permitted the Crisis Management Team to understand the situation

➤ Effectiveness of countermeasures applied to limit the event's progress

➤ Coordination with public agencies and effectiveness

➤ Effectiveness of internal communications about the event

➤ Effectiveness of external communications about it

➤ Efforts and effectiveness to restore business operations

➤ Recovery: degree of return to pre-event levels and when achieved

➤ Mitigation recommendations to limit future impacts

➤ Opportunities that resulted from this event

➤ Estimated date the event can be closed

➤ Attachments: narratives of key participants, especially their recommendations for improvements — the Lessons Learned List

Undoubtedly, much of the data should be marked company confidential, with limited distribution. However, those parts that can be widely circulated should be, lest opportunities to improve response management, reduce costs, and shorten recovery time be lost. Loss of those opportunities would invite justifiable criticism.

■ DISCLAIMER

For readers who see this chapter's technological aspects some time after publication, I ask you to remember that the rate of change for communications technology as of this writing in the spring of 2002 is both dizzying and accelerating.

Appendix A: Emergency Response Team Candidate Selection Survey

RESPONSE TEAM CANDIDATE PROFILE

MEDICAL AND FIRST AID TRAINING

First Aid

    [ ] Standard   [ ] Current

    [ ] Advanced   [ ] Date last qualified _____

    [ ] Instructor

Emergency Medical Technician

    [ ] EMT-1A or -1FS   [ ] Current

    [ ] EMT-II   [ ] Date last qualified _____

    [ ] EMT-P

Nursing

    [ ] RN   List specialty/experience _____

    [ ] LVN   Specialty/experience _____

LAW ENFORCEMENT AND RELATED EXPERIENCE

    [ ] Former police officer   [ ] Security officer

    [ ] Reserve officer

    [ ] Military police or security

    [ ] Other _____

FIRE AND RESCUE SERVICES

    [ ] Paid firefighter   [ ] Reserve/volunteer fire-fighter

    [ ] Rescue squad/ambulance   [ ] Light/medium rescue training

    [ ] Heavy rescue training   [ ] SAR team

COMMUNICATIONS

    [ ] Amateur   [ ] CB   [ ] Public Safety Dispatcher

[ ] Military   [ ] Telephone operator/
                              answering service
[ ] Messenger/runner [ ] Other _____

SURVIVAL TRAINING OR EXPERIENCE

[ ] Course(s) and date(s) _____

LANGUAGE SKILLS

[ ] Language _____ [ ] translator [ ] read/write
[ ] Language _____ [ ] translator [ ] read/write

VEHICLE AVAILABILITY AT WORK OR WITHIN WALKING DISTANCE

Please list the vehicles you own/use that could be useful in emergencies.

[ ] 4WD   [ ] RV   [ ] Trail bike
                     [ ] Bicycle   (motorcycle)
[ ] Street motorcycle [ ] Minivan   [ ] Pickup

EMERGENCY EXPERIENCE

Please explain, as "1989 San Francisco earthquake", etc.

_____

_____

MECHANICAL OR CONSTRUCTION ABILITIES

[ ] Carpentry   [ ] Electrical
[ ] Plumbing   [ ] Auto repair

CHILD OR ELDER CARE TRAINING

[ ] Church nursery   [ ] Day care facility—kids
[ ] Day care facility—elderly [ ] Other _____
Please give dates and number of wards:

_____

_____

OTHER

Are you a member of an emergency service organization, or do you have related special training not covered above?

_____

_____

NAME _____

    Mail routing _____

    Email address _____

    Office phone _____

    Home zip code _____

    Dept. Head's name _____

Appendix B: Media Policy during Major Emergencies

MEDIA POLICY DURING MAJOR EMERGENCIES

During any emergency involving OurCo, we should expect considerable attention to focus on our corporation through the media. The confidence in OurCo held by our clients, investors, and others will reflect the image that we present under stress. It is important that we show how the foresight, preparation, and practice that this firm's management and all employees have invested result in fewer casualties, less damage, and the ability to maintain business as usual.

➤ Media inquiries will be referred to a single spokesperson, who is the [*fill in appropriate manager's title here*]. In his or her absence, the Chief Executive Officer will select an alternate.

➤ A media center will be provided to keep members of the working press out of the weather and hazardous areas. Such amenities as are available will be provided, including water, restrooms, chairs, and telephones.

➤ All members of the media will be afforded even-handed treatment. No favoritism or individual restrictions will be applied.

➤ Members of the media will not be permitted into hazardous areas or where emergency response activities are in progress, such as firefighting, rescues, or first aid treatment.

➤ Where sufficient media interest has been generated so that large numbers of the media would be disruptive, one pool cameraperson and one reporter from the electronic media and one pool reporter and one cameraperson from the print media will be taken on a tour of the area by the OurCo spokesperson, accompanied by OurCo personnel with sufficient expertise to answer anticipated questions. The pool media persons are to be selected by the media representatives present, not by OurCo employees.

➤ Interviews with key OurCo personnel will be facilitated at the discretion of the individual and on a not-to-interfere basis with essential response and recovery functions.

➤ The privacy of individual OurCo employees and their families will be respected. The names of deceased and injured OurCo employees will not be released by OurCo unless their families have been notified or the individual concerned has authorized such release. Their complete addresses will not be made public, although their hometowns or districts may be, as well as the names of any hospitals to which employees have been taken. Interviews with the injured or employees in highly emotional states will not be permitted on OurCo premises.

➤ Information released will contain only facts and such positive information as is available. Speculations, causal factors that resulted in disruptive events or emergencies, or attempts to fix responsibility or blame on individuals or organizations will not be included in public statements. Releases will be written whenever practicable, with copies provided for each media representative present, and will be handed out with prepared press kits to include:

  ➤ A backgrounder on OurCo and its operations
  ➤ A backgrounder on the OurCo disaster avoidance program

➤ Media inquiries, whether by electronic means or in person, will be answered as directly as is practical. Where the information is not known or not releasable under this policy, the media representative will be noted and a response provided as soon as practical.

MEDIA POLICY DURING MAJOR EMERGENCIES

LIMITED DISTRIBUTION

This is a supplement to MEDIA POLICY DURING MAJOR EMERGENCIES. This supplement is for distribution only to those OurCo employees whose duties will include direct contact with reporters: Board of Directors Members, Senior Managers, and members of the Corporate Communications staff.

The purpose of this supplement is to avoid mistakes made by other organizations under stress. Those kinds of mistakes reduce an individual's credibility or reduce a community's confidence in those organizations.

➤ Prepare by taking notes addressing who, what, when, where, why, and how *within our media policy.* Speak from those notes.

➤ Do not editorialize and risk distorting facts with words such as "terrible," "bloody," and so on. Any fatality or major injury is, and should be referred to as, a "tragedy," or "tragic".

➤ Never lie.

➤ It is not necessary to reveal a fact that may compromise confidence in OurCo.

➤ In the event that discovery of such a fact is imminent, it is better to reveal it before discovery if at all practical.

➤ When you do not know, say so, and ask how to contact the media representative when you can find out. Be sure to follow up on your promise.

➤ When asked a rhetorical question with negative implications, such as "When will you admit OurCo's negligence caused this?" an indirect true answer can be effective, such as "OurCo's pledge to this community is to conduct operations as safe as humans can make them. We will investigate thoroughly and find what did cause this."

➤ You need not answer every question in the terms of the questioner. "How many of your people died here today?" could be answered with "The fire service's paramedics take those with injuries beyond minor to hospitals, and it's too soon to hear back from them."

Appendix C: Internal Information during Major Emergencies

During any major disruptive event involving OurCo, we can expect our employees and others on our premises to want to know as much as possible about what has happened and what will happen—to them, to their jobs, and to their families. This is especially true in a regional or targeted event, such as an earthquake, prolonged storm, tornado, or explosion, when there is obvious damage to structures around them with injured people, and so on.

It is the duty of the OurCo [*fill in appropriate manager's title here*] and staff to provide them with facts without delay or embellishment. The [*manager's title*] may form information teams to deliver factual information.

Use these guidelines:

➤ The [*manager's title*] has responsibility and authority to clear all information being furnished to OurCo's employees.

➤ Determine who, what, when, where, why, and how. This information should be available from the Plans and Intelligence Manager in the Crisis Management Center.

➤ Tell what you know, what is not yet known, and what's being done. Avoid speculation about causal factors, or who bears responsibility or blame as individuals or organizations.

➤ Post the information on the password-protected part of OurCo's Web site for employees and on the employees' call-in 800 number and give it to the call center operators for release to employees only. Where electronic systems are not functioning, have their managers

gather employees in groups and deliver the information face to face.

➤ Answer questions honestly. If something that our employees want to know is unknown, admit it and try to
have an information team member get back.

➤ Do not give names of injured or dead persons. Your information must be truthful. OurCo employees will
know that others have been injured. Give numbers, if
known, and the fact that OurCo's Emergency Response Teams are giving the injured good care.

Emphasize the positive. OurCo has a well-organized, practiced disaster avoidance and crisis management program.
Establish a routine to deliver frequent updates to employees.

Chapter 6

Today, Business Is Different

■ PREVIOUS DISASTER COUNTERMEASURES ALONE ARE NO LONGER ADEQUATE

It isn't just the faster pace of business that makes previous disaster recovery planning inadequate, although the faster pace is real enough. The greater reality is that companies must continue to take the conventional steps against threats that can escalate into disasters, *plus* other actions. What are those other actions?

➤ Insurance since September 11, 2001

One of the principal changes is that the insurance industry has recognized terrorism as a risk to themselves, both directly as targets and indirectly against their continuance as a financial base for other industries' recoveries. In the latter regard, insurers have reevaluated their positions—just as they did after the one-two punches of Hurricanes Andrew and Iniki, then another one-two combination from the Kobe and Northridge earthquakes. Those double combinations brought the realization that several known threats could materialize into realities within a relatively short time, and that the increase in insured losses during the 1990–2000 decade were small compared to losses that could come from potential future disasters.[1] When the primary insurers consulted with their own backups (the reinsurance companies), they discovered that the primary reinsurers were also aware of the potentials, and they realized specifically that the primary insurance and reinsurance industries in the United States have only approximately $245 billion of capital to service catastrophe claims that could easily reach $50 billion. That could wipe out something over 20 percent of their capital,[2] which would devastate the industry.[3] To no one's great surprise, the insurance industry has reacted by reducing or eliminating terrorism coverage from commercial policies for many industries.[4]

At risk of stating the obvious, one of the other actions that corporations thinking about avoiding disasters should do without delay is communicate in writing with their casualty insurers about the terrorism scenarios that proved to be realistic when they went through their risk analyses (the guidelines for which are in Chapter 2). Corporations should ask insurers whether they are still covered and whether the amount of coverage *specific to losses from terrorist acts* is adequate, given the new face of terrorism worldwide.

The almost-good news is that many insurers are still offering terrorism insurance, though as separate policies and with a greater total cost. Communication with the company's insurer should not be limited to acts of terrorism but should include threats from natural causes. The loss trends from nature's disruptive events have been rising over time because of a number of factors. I also recommend inquiring about the adequacy of business continuity coverage for accidental causes because surveys of managers report that, after power outages, information systems (ISs) are most at risk from employee errors and hardware and software failures.[5] These impacts put today's businesses that rely more on digital inputting, data processing, electronic data storage, and computerized production more at risk than businesses that in the past conducted mainly over-the-counter and paperwork-train transactions.

■ THE ELECTRONIC SPEEDS OF DIGITAL PROCESSING REQUIRE FASTER EVENT RECOGNITION

The revolution of digital electronic inputting, processing, and recording business operations and their supporting functions not only changed the rate at which ongoing business is conducted; it also raised the expectations of customers, employees, suppliers, senior management, regulators, and the media — all of whom are people who connect with companies to conduct business. Expectations are that telephones will be answered within four rings, that whoever you are talking to can pull up your account history in 10 seconds, that he or she is empowered to give you an answer or put you through to someone who can in under a minute, and so forth (with the paradoxical exception of most computer-related companies' customer services divisions).

Because digital systems operating at the speed of light make all those accelerations in business processes practical, they also permit a single point of failure to become a chain-reaction systems crash at the same speed. And although systems engineers install cutouts to stop chain-reaction crashes automatically, they do not always work. In fact, such failures are common enough to have brought their impacts into the professional lexicon. We speak of *compound emergencies*. One of the consequences is that readers responsible for developing plans to avoid disasters should also be concerned with alerting systems that can get their Crisis Management Team functioning *without delay*.

"Without delay" might seem to be an unnecessary emphasis, but it is not. To understand why not, the characteristics common to most crises should be enlightening.

■ ANATOMY OF A CRISIS

Major disruptive events often go unrecognized at first. The reasons are based in our human experiences:

➤ First reports may sound routine.

➤ Callers seldom convey the event's scope.

➤ Potential consequences may not be apparent early on.

Crises develop *very* rapidly. As just described, when cutouts do not work, digital systems crash simultaneously — far too fast for human intervention. Compounding that situation, the digital revolution's speed of information transfer makes it likely that reporters, employees, investors, and other important stakeholders will learn about events as quickly as your Crisis Management Team does.

Other things the new speeds of today's business have produced that challenge disaster avoidance planners include the raised expectations just mentioned. All those important stakeholders *as well as* senior management (!) will expect your Crisis Management Team to get the picture very quickly, to stay informed as information develops, and to begin making decisions that will limit further damage and restart business functions at almost the same speed. Chapter 7 deals more with the issues surrounding restarting. For now, let us continue to examine the anatomy of a crisis.

Crises require policy-level involvement early on. Summarizing earlier statements, there were three reasons for policy-level executives to become directly involved beyond simply monitoring developments:

1. When the company's crisis management capabilities are not yet developed, those executives usually have the most background and experience.

2. When a situation arises for which no policy guidance is yet established, they usually have the best chance to make policy as the event unfolds.

3. When a situation arises that could cause grave damage to the company, they are often the group most likely to recognize it and to counter it.

Given the speed of travel for news (accurate or not) in today's digital environment, there is also a fourth reason:

4. When the issues surfacing require high visibility appearances by policy-level executives.

No doubt readers will recall events involving consumer product safety in which the manufacturers' CEOs were "too busy" to appear before Congressional investigation committees and their phalanxes of news media's cameras. Early alerts and briefings for those executives plus their visibility can reduce lost confidence among investors, customers, regulators, and members of the public who know little more than the brand names.

Monitoring, as opposed to direct involvement, should be done by at least one policy-level executive as soon as practical during a disruptive event to ensure that established policies are being adhered to and to detect the development of a situation that could cause the grave damage just warned of.

Another characteristic of a crisis is that although good decision making requires a flow of information that is plentiful, accurate, and focused, the first reports are likely to be fragmented. And with partial and sometimes inaccurate information in hand, decision times arrive—much sooner than the Crisis Management Team would wish.

■ CRISIS COUNTERMEASURES IN THE DIGITAL ENVIRONMENT'S TIME FRAME

To overcome the lack of early recognition, build alerting systems. In 24-7 businesses, the call center is often the first line of defense. Its operators need a list of criteria that require a supervisor to be brought on line to evaluate the situation, and the supervisors need to know that there is no penalty for alerting managers if the event does not develop into a crisis. Disaster avoidance planners should understand that there will be only one confidence check at that level. The first time a manager receives a midnight alert, every call center supervisor will hear what the reaction was.

In businesses with more traditional working hours, the first line is usually the late-shift managers or the company's security services, who are often a contractor's employees. In smaller businesses, the public safety agencies become their surrogates. No matter who the first line of defense is, the same alerting criteria should apply, and for the same reasons.

Once the alerting messages are received, the company's Crisis Management Center need not be fully staffed until it is apparent that the event will develop into a crisis. Such centers need activation stages, from "Wait and Watch," through "Gather Data and Begin Planning," into "All Hands at Work." Because crises develop today at digital speeds, a tiered and very quick team-alerting call-up system that matches the time challenge is a requirement, and so are backup systems to ensure reliability.

The need for policy-level involvement has been discussed; therefore, the alerting system should extend to alerting a senior management representative who is responsible for deciding when to notify the policy-level executives above him or her. Although a senior management representative need not be *involved* in the "Wait and Watch" stage of activation, he or she *should* be notified early in the chain of developments, if only to be sure that the communications linkages are in place. The Crisis Management Team's leader is then assured that contact can be resumed very quickly if activation goes beyond an early stage.

In summary, today's pace of business means that emergencies can escalate at that pace, so the crisis management structure's ability to mobilize should match it with an ability to activate and deactivate quickly, both in stages.

■ A NOTE ABOUT SELECTING ACTIVATION STAGES

While I know much about the sequence that allows disruptive events to enter that graveyard spiral that can terminate as a catastrophe and about ways to interrupt the sequence, however, you are the only one who knows how your company's business functions. It follows that I can only offer generic

> More steps = more complication = less understanding.

guidelines and an example of Crisis Management Team and Crisis Management Center activation criteria. You should then adapt those to the company's specific operations.

To begin, I recommend keeping it simple. A good idea is to remember who is going to have to implement activation early in the event, with limited staffing and little practice. Beyond that, here are some generic guidelines:

➤ Stage 1
  ➤ *Criterion:* A disruptive event is reported that has the capability of escalating enough to disrupt ongoing operations.

➤ *Actions:* 1. Alert the Crisis Management Team. 2. Bring in the plans and intelligence manager and the team leader. 3. Activate their parts of the Crisis Management Center.[6] 4. Establish solid communications with the scene, including backups. 5. Alert the managers responsible for the impacted business operations. 6. Consider putting a highly reliable representative on scene.

➤ Stage 2

➤ *Criterion:* Operations are interrupted, or they will be.

➤ *Actions:* 1. Inform the senior management representative. 2. Activate the physical Crisis Management Center. 3. Put a reliable representative at the scene. 4. Bring in the plans and intelligence manager's assistant and the team leader's assistant. 5. Bring in the other Center functional managers. 6. Bring in the public relations assistant. 7. Alert the other staff assistants to the team leader.

➤ Stage 3

➤ *Criterion:* Critical business unit operations are interrupted and are expected to remain down for longer than the end of the unit's business cycle.

➤ *Actions:* 1. Bring in all members of the Crisis Management Team. 2. Notify all employees that the Team is up and running. Remind them that the Team is not to be pumped for information and that updates will be posted via e-mail and other standard channels. Remind them that the Team may call on any employee for his or her expertise to help the Team resolve issues related to the event.

Thinking about alerting guidelines, readers will have discovered that they may need different criteria for different operations. That is very likely to be true for different sites and their differing threats. Here is an example for a manufacturing operation:

Initial report. A distant plant's shift supervisor reports that a lightning strike caused a fire during his minimally staffed midnight shift. The plant's Emergency Response Team has extinguished the fire, and there are no personnel casualties. Damage assessment is in progress, and the plant's manager is en route from home. *Response:* Initiate Crisis Management Team's Stage 1 and request the plant's manager call when a preliminary damage assessment is in hand.

Second report. The plant's manager calls to advise that fire damage will stop production on the only line for a high-revenue product until a new part can be installed. She requests assistance locating a replacement part and reports that when the part is flown in, production can resume in one working day. *Response:* Activate Crisis Management Team's Stage 2 with the full logistics section and notify the executive responsible for that plant's product.

Additional information. Two of the company's customers use that plant's product in their brands of a consumer product. They are locked in a market-share war over that consumer product. The manufacturer of the part that the plant needs advises that the part must be manufactured, with earliest availability in 30 days. One of the customers has a 20-day supply of the needed parts on hand. The other customer has a five-day supply and is reviewing its legal options if the plant cannot deliver by then. *Response:* Initiate Stage 3 and request that senior management obtain policy-level guidance while the Crisis Management Team prepares an analysis of the alternatives.

It is not always necessary to work up through the sequence as was done in the previous example. In fact, the criteria were provided to encourage training Crisis Management Teams to go directly to an appropriate stage and putting the needed resources in play without becoming process driven. It follows that when solutions have been implemented, the stages can be used again to wind down the crisis management operation efficiently.

■ BUSINESS CONTINUITY STRATEGIES

Part of planning to avoid disasters in today's business environment includes selecting strategies in advance to be used for restoring specific business functions, services, or product lines. There are five general options, but before discussing them, I would like to share my view of an underlying concept.

In few instances are absolute numbers the most useful way to define and consider outages or downtimes. One of the seminal articles that focused managers' thinking on disasters and how to overcome them was written almost 20 years ago, and it focused readers in part on customers' expectations. In the *Harvard Business Review,* Virgil Dissmeyer related how the effects of a fire that all but destroyed the headquarters of a major bank and its parent company's headquarters, with their associated customer services,[7] were allayed by adapting an existing severe weather plan, as well as by the fact that the event occurred on Thanksgiving Day. Because the next regular business day was Monday, there were three full days to restore the high-visibility business functions. Northwestern National Bank of Minneapolis made excellent use of that time, and that article first got me thinking about customers' expectations as another way to measure downtime. That fact provides opportunities to make disaster avoidance planning less expensive and more efficient by matching restoration strategies to customers' expectations.

There are some notable exceptions to the concept that customers' expectations are usually a better way to determine how much time, toil, and treasure to expend on restoring specific business functions. Some of those exceptions are when trading is 24-7, when lives are at risk, and when processes can become physically unstable with the potential for disastrous results. Having noted some exceptions, let us now discuss the five choices for strategies.

■ STRATEGY 1: ELIMINATING THE THREAT

The first option, and usually the most cost-beneficial, is to eliminate the threat. That almost always requires an operational change or partnering with an outside organization, depending on who owns the threat. In one instance, an extremely dangerous chemical was eliminated from a manufacturing operation. It took a near catastrophe to change enough minds within the company and accomplish that, but that is one way, regardless. Where an outside organization owns the threat, it almost always takes a very long time and requires more than one group seeking change. That makes this first and most cost-beneficial option least likely to be accomplished in an acceptable time frame. Either approach to this strategy should be considered as a long-term solution while the following three are being applied to buy time.

■ STRATEGY 2: CONTINUITY

The second strategy is business process *continuity*, which goes by other names depending on the industry involved.

Electric power distributors refer to no-break power systems; computers processing in tandem are called paralleling; and duplicated communications paths with automatic switching are ironically spoken of as redundant systems. I prefer the term *continuity* because it focuses on the purpose for the strategy. Again, the concept should be considered from the viewpoint of the customers — including other business functions within the company in the definition of customers.

Using the lightning-strike scenario just mentioned, if there were sufficient product on hand to continue shipments until production could be restored, that would satisfy the requirements of a continuity strategy. Of course, with the financial services industry, storing product is not an option, which brings up an aspect of such services that deserves discussion. It may make sense to have more than one strategy for the same product line.

If an inability to trade securities that develops after close of business can be restored before trading opens the next business day, that would satisfy the requirement for business continuity. If that same ability is lost during trading hours, any restoration plan that takes more than a few minutes can result in serious losses. Entirely aside from direct financial costs, the lost confidence in certain industries (financial, health care, and anything moving at or above freeway speeds come immediately to mind) reflects additional costs to which few brand managers would consent. The same is true of the increased costs that additional regulation brings in the wake of lost confidence. There are additional impacts, which are listed and described in Appendix A of Chapter 4. The point for this discussion is that when selecting strategies, achieving a balance between direct financial costs and the benefits from reducing those impacts requires careful consideration and discussion with other managers who will have to deal with the specific types of impacts.

■ STRATEGY 3: QUICK RESTORATION DISASTER RECOVERY

This third strategy accepts downtime through the normal close of the current business cycle or another short period acceptable to an industry's customers. The key to this strategy is usually nearly instant resource availability and transportation support. Where sources of supplies, equipment, services, specialized requirements, and transportation can be galvanized, this strategy can be effective with reasonable costs. A common way to achieve this is through *alternate work sites* (AWSs), a term that is replacing *cold* or *hot sites*. At a cold site, a vacant contracted space assumed to match the company's needs is ready and maintained by a contractor who agrees to provide instant availability—to the company that calls first. The company's critical business units' software and databases can be brought there to be quickly loaded, so processing can proceed within a day or two. Some cold sites can have a processor matching the company's installed and operating within days. As the processor is being brought up, workstations for the critical business units are connected either from the company's offices or from another precontracted location. Hot sites, on the other hand, have a matching processor on the premises and may have the software applications there also, which decreases the time to resume interactive processing after current databases can be accessed.

The methods for these forms of business restoration, often lumped under the term *disaster recovery,* are changing. As more contractors respond to demand for many more such sites closer to companies' usual operating locations, stand-alone processors at distant sites are becoming less common than those that include numerous workstations in the same building, and they are being built nearer where companies are clustered (and employees live). The terminology now coming into common use (AWS) reflects that development.

When comparing the costs of different strategies, a handy mnemonic is the *three Ts*: time, toil, and treasure, reflecting their more quantifiable bases of time to restore, person-hours, and financial costs. This third strategy of quick restoration may intuitively seem to be considerably less costly than the previous strategy of business continuity, but that may not be true if disruptive events occur frequently. The reason is that although the systems that are put in place to ensure business continuity have a high initial cost, they seldom recur, aside from reasonable testing and maintenance. Quick restoration using an alternate work site is labor intensive and involves shifting many highly paid people from their usual tasks into a very intense restoration endeavor involving installation, task changes, database transmission, and testing—and then shifting them back, to restore operations at a permanent location and catch up with their usual work. That effort is costly in itself, and if that cycle is repeated within a period of two to three years, decreased employee morale and retention add to the costs.

■ STRATEGY 4: DEFERRED RESTORATION DISASTER RECOVERY

A fourth strategy is to restore operations sometime after the first business day, or after the company's short-term business cycle. This strategy is workable for business functions whose customers are less impacted by the longer restoration times. In today's business environment, not many of the business units with direct customer contact can tolerate restoration on those terms, but those that can will facilitate considerably reduced costs in all of the three Ts.

A note of caution about planning to use this strategy: Remember the earlier point about my mistake in believing the bank's trust department when they told me that they need not be included in the groups served by the quick restoration strategy. Fortunately, the story of the trust instrument and First Interstate's fire surfaced before any real damage was done, except for a few red faces. A second cautionary note is that restoration strategies should match changed circumstances. One thing a Crisis Management Team should do during any emergency that can persist is contact the business units that are programmed for lower priority recoveries to verify that delayed recovery is still acceptable.

■ STRATEGY 5: DISCONTINUING THE PRODUCT

The fifth strategy is to discontinue the product or service. While that may seem to be an unlikely action at first consideration, in any large organization some products, brands, or services may be scheduled for discontinuation in the company's strategic planning. The opportunity to accelerate the discontinuation date may arrive early with an outage. There are costs associated with this action, and they should be compared with the costs of restoration.

■ EXPLAINING STRATEGY DEVELOPMENT

There is a relatively uncomplicated way to create a graphic showing why a specific business unit is matched to a strategy (see Figure 6.1). It uses the responses of the business units' managers when given the scenarios that have both high intensities and high return rates. The business units' managers respond with their estimates of those scenarios' impacts on their units' contributions to the company's production and profitability.

Looking at Figure 6.1, the three business units in the upper-right quadrant reported that the scenarios would have severe impacts on their production and that their lost contributions to the company's profitability would also have relatively large impacts. They then become logical candidates for the company's critical business units — candidates for the business continuity or quick restoration strategies.

For companies in which the corporate culture embraces mathematical proofs, the business units' managers estimates of all seven impacts might be quantified, an algorithm developed, and its solutions offered to substantiate the identification of critical business units and the selection of restoration strategies. However, I recall discussions of significant digits during statistics courses and suspect that such

PRODUCTION IMPACT

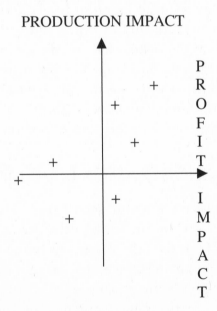

Figure 6.1 Matching Specific Business Units to Strategies

exertions would offend my professors, who warned against showing solutions that appeared to offer greater accuracy than the initial SWAG ("some wild approximate guess") data would make possible.

■ TESTING

Chapter 3 included considerable discussion about exercises that test plans while training management teams. This section expands that discussion to note additional testing requirements that e-businesses have.

The additional requirements are brought on in part by the 24-7 nature of e-business. Because of that pace, outages (and impairments that have the impacts of outages) can put the company's market share at risk. Because of the way call centers are staffed, employees need clear, foolproof instructions to help them recognize outages and other emergencies, and they need clear criteria about when and how to make notifications. That is critical because unless and until those notifications occur, management will not be able to work the problem. So, what to test?

The first item for testing is *readability*. The issue is whether the implementers can quickly grasp what they must do. Having the writer review the instructions will not help much. He or she knows what the implementers are supposed to do and thinks that it is written so that they will understand and do those things. As with the instructions for more traditional business operations, it is good practice to remember who is going to be the company's first line of defense. For the traditional businesses, it could be the minimally staffed midnight shift supervisor or a security officer patrolling an idling plant. For a 24-7 e-business, it may well be the shift supervisor at a call center. A good preliminary test would be to take the draft instructions to just such a person and ask, "If [the triggering event] happens, what would you do?" to get a critique. After the instructions are in the field, checking to be sure that they become part of the implementers' training—including frequent reinforcement—should be part of preparing to avoid disaster.

The second item for testing is *integration*. Do the people responsible for key emergency management functions know when and how to coordinate? Using an earlier example, do the company's Emergency Response Teams understand that the first real data in an accident or natural disaster will come from them? Does the plans and intelligence manager on the Crisis Management Team know that the Team's public relations manager needs periodic updates? Does the IS representative on the Team realize that those systems provide the feedback about how customers are responding, almost minute by minute, to the disruptive event? And do the call center operators understand that they become the company's points of contact to collect customer responses?

When preparing tests of those information chains, many exercise preparations have a sequence something like, "Ready! Fire! Aim!" Thinking about constructing exercises for tests and training, the "Aim!" part is choosing the objectives and making them known to the exercise's participants. A scenario that will "fire" to facilitate achieving those objectives comes *after* objectives are developed.

Testing objectives can include validations. Are there orderly transitions between steps? Recognition of a potentially disruptive event should lead to alerting and monitoring. Monitoring a situation that develops into such an event should lead to notification, then to response management, restoring critical business operations, and so on—which lead us into the next chapter. However, there are two more points for discussion about testing.

The first is that testing should include validating the adequacy of resources. The scenario should be crafted to discover whether the required skills, space, hardware, supplies, software, transportation, and specialized items can be brought to bear quickly and in the required quantities.

Finally, perhaps the most important thing about testing and training—especially in the digitally fast business environment where specialized knowledge is essential—is the participants' feedback. Their Lessons Learned Lists provide the recommendations for increasing the company's probability of avoiding disaster.

Chapter 7

Recovery Is Really Different

■ SEPTEMBER 11, 2001: THE RULES GOT REWRITTEN—OR DID THEY?

No terrorist act within the United States before September 11, 2001, demonstrated such close coordination on that day's scale; nor was one aimed at such high-visibility symbols of corporate enterprise, then carried out with such utter disregard for the lives of either the perpetrators or their victims. In the planning for that day, the rules for terrorists were indeed rewritten, and with them the rules for recovery have changed.

That September 11 also brought the first necessity for the United States military forces, local government response agencies, and businesses' recovery resources to work simultaneously on an immense scale.[1] From now on, the need for all three to work in coordination rivaling that of the terrorists is surely apparent. Changing mindsets and organizing to facilitate that coordination should be part of the tasks of executives responsible for avoiding disasters.

However, not everything changed.

■ THE DEFINITION OF RECOVERY DID NOT CHANGE, BUT ITS RULES DID

Recovery is still considered one of the phases in business

continuity planning and emergency or crisis management. Nominally, recovery is the phase between response and mitigation, but there are no distinct lines denoting a time when response is over and recovery has begun. In fact, in several highly effective Crisis Management Centers there is a managerial position responsible for recovery issues, and those Centers are not considered fully staffed until that position is filled during the response phase.[2] I recommend following those excellent examples and organizing your Crisis Management Center to include a recovery position.

Just as recovery actions should begin during the response phase, they continue well into the time when mitigation activities are underway. The transition lines from response to recovery to mitigation are blurred at best.[3] Perhaps thinking of overlapping zones is a better management metaphor.

■ THE REQUIREMENTS FOR RECOVERY INFORMATION DID NOT CHANGE

Something else that didn't change on September 11 is the recovery phase manager's need for quality information. In common with the response phase especially, incomplete information is part of any manager's reality — with a couple of "howevers" about recovery information.

> ➤ *However 1:* Managers working on recovery issues have more time to get the information than the managers during the response phase did.

> ➤ *However 2:* Incoming information becomes harder to verify.

The principal reason for both statements is that during the recovery phase, the issues relate more to opinions, and single-interest groups bring their agendas to be addressed as part of the recovery process. There will be more discussion about this phenomenon, with real-world illustrations, later in this chapter.

■ RECOVERY IS NOT RESTORATION

Another thing that can be confusing is that we are now discussing *long-term recovery* with many strategic issues, and it is difficult to stop thinking about short-term *restoration* issues. One of the things that changes during recovery is that companies that were not only willing but also eager to assist one another with mutual aid during the response phase and on into restoration will now move back to their more normal competitive postures and become less willing to share resources. The same is true for divisions within companies. During the response phase in the Crisis Management Center, the underlying concept was *integrated emergency management.* With the Center's activity slowing down, the silos (or stovepipes) isolating the divisions inside companies will be coming back, and this will lead to two different time periods that managers should understand as they work to obtain and implement recovery ideas to facilitate avoiding repeat disasters.

■ THE MANAGER'S WINDOWS OF OPPORTUNITY

There are two different windows of opportunity. However, comparing those time periods to the windows of a building is somewhat misleading because periods of opportunity for change do not resemble windows that stay in place. Managers should think of a period of opportunity as an open door on a passing train. It is not very wide, and it is moving all the time. Wise managers will be prepared with items in need of change gleaned from Lessons Learned Lists and from their risk analyses even before the lessons from a real event are collected.

The first opportunity occurs immediately after the disruptive event, when nearly everyone can focus on the event, its impact still seems real, and they can believe another such event is likely to recur. Often, a business unit's manager who has reviewed the risk analysis will support the proposed changes to reduce his or her business unit's vulnerability. The open door of opportunity is in range; the disaster avoidance manager has an ally; and senior management has just seen a real-world event. Update the business case for risk reduction and seize the opportunity.

The second opportunity occurs when outside agencies review regional events. Task forces are often formed, and community inputs are sought. Where a public-private partnership to address disaster preparedness is already in place, a company's disaster avoidance manager will be wise to get representation on it and advocate improvements that can reduce the company's vulnerability while benefiting the community. That is especially true for infrastructure improvements, many of which require receptive minds among the utility companies or public works agencies.

Where there is no public-private partnership in place, seeking time on the agenda of the nearly inevitable investigative body that will be required to draft new laws, regulations, and standards is a good example of strategic thinking. Here again, the time of opportunity — though it passes by a little later — is transitory and brief. I recommend adding the formation of a public-private partnership against disasters to one's to-do list. There are a number of success stories with long-term benefits linked to that achievement. More on that in the next chapter.

■ PLAN REVISIONS FROM LESSONS LEARNED

One thing that is almost assured in the recovery phase is getting the plan revised, and that is another thing September 11 reaffirmed. As the disruptive event begins to wind down, collect the participants' recommendations for improvement—the Lessons Learned List—just as you would after a simulation exercise. Collate the ideas and begin making the changes that can be accomplished without coordination. Begin immediately with those that may require a great deal of coordination ("salesmanship"). There are two reasons for this recommendation: First the most efficient use of time to accomplish changes is to get the long-timeline ones started; in addition, while the other managers to be convinced are pondering their value, starting those changes that require less coordination will allow many changes to be completed at about the same time. The second reason is that the opportunity may be at hand—but it will not be for long.

The underlying reason for trying to accelerate implementing improvements evoked from either experience or simulations is that the next disruptive event is drawing closer while changes are being negotiated. Hark, footsteps!

■ PEOPLE ARE NUMBER ONE ... NO, REALLY!

People who plan to avoid disasters have been saying and repeating that axiom like a mantra to their colleagues in other parts of their companies for at least the past 10 years. Whenever planning is discussed among professionals, that statement is very likely to be emphasized. And then they sigh, because most professionals know that the basic elements necessary for protecting employees and returning them to productivity without undue delay have been understood and recommended from the time that management's focus changed from life safety drills to disaster recovery, and that remains with us as today's managers focus on business continuity. Still, the foundation for protecting people seldom gets put in place—at least, it is nothing like the full underpinning.

One thing that September 11 brought home is the truth of the idea that people are number one. It didn't change, but perhaps many companies began to believe it for the first time.

Rick Rescorla, vice president of security for Morgan Stanley Dean Witter, understood that the World Trade Center's risks of and vulnerability to terrorist attack would endanger his company's number one asset: its people. He planned for complete evacuation of Morgan Stanley's people on its 30 floors of the south tower. He implemented evacuation drills of pairs walking down the stairs, which readers will understand required considerable coordination ("salesmanship") with both the company's senior management and building management (Port Authority) security. When the 1993 garage bombing occurred, every Morgan Stanley employee made it out, and Morgan Stanley's planning and training were no longer disputable. When September 11 arrived, Rescorla knew that the admonitions to remain in place would, if heeded, increase the risk to the company's people. He implemented the evacuation plan again. All but six of the company's 2,700 people survived. Rescorla was last seen returning up the stairs to clear stragglers.[4]

What should be done to help protect the company's most valuable asset? Following are the essentials:

➤ Self-protection instruction

➤ Family preparedness information

➤ Site Emergency Response Teams

➤ Employee crisis information line or e-mail

➤ Evacuation and relocation drills that include safe assembly area instructions and postevacuation employee accounting

All of those are inexpensive, have high employee-relations paybacks, and will help your company get back into operation before the competition. Other companies did not have a Rick Rescorla and thus were not so fortunate,[5] which brings us to the second part of the people issue.

September 11 made managers revisit the fact that some key people may no longer be present in a crisis.[6] During exercises and the discussions that precede them, that issue should be broached. In some organizations, managers with similar roles at other sites can be brought in to help fill the gaps. Government emergency managers call them Overhead Teams. For other organizations, the solutions may be unique to their situations. During management training exercises, one reason for a Simulation Group is unobtrusive training. When participants become familiar with exercising as training, switching the primary functional managers with their counterparts from the Simulation Group instills confidence among Senior Managers (and provides opportunities for mild joshing among colleagues).

■ PREPARE FOR THE OTHER CASUALTIES

Another thing that will not change is this: Some employees will be so affected by the stresses of the event that their performances will become impaired. This foreseeable occurrence, which is denied or denigrated by some, can be diminished with recognition and treatment. Without treatment, it has resulted in the departure of 30 percent to 50 percent of an organization's management staff within three years[7] of major events. The techniques to identify at-risk employees and then to lessen their accumulated stress are beyond the scope of this book. From a manager's viewpoint, it is enough to know that those impacts are real and can be ameliorated. Please see Chapter 11 for more information.

■ THE "AVOID GEOGRAPHIC CONCENTRATION" RULE

Within a month of September 11, Morgan Stanley announced the sale of its nearly completed office tower in midtown Manhattan and its plans to move several thousand employees outside New York City.[8] On the day of the terrorist attacks, many companies learned that by contracting with a single telecommunications provider, they had made themselves vulnerable to what reliability engineers and disaster avoidance professionals refer to as a *single point of failure*. Geographic concentration of a company's vital assets or critical business functions is something that business continuity professionals warn against, so that's another "not new" item from September 11, coupled to some new items. The new items? One difference is that companies are changing their behaviors. Another difference is that we now know that those concentrations will exacerbate the impacts of terrorist events. A third difference is that the traditional separation between a company's usual business site and the corresponding alternate work site must now be increased, placing the alternate work site on a different power grid and using different communications switches.

■ ORGANIZE!

The topic of organizing for long-term corporate business recovery has not been extensively studied with the classic four-step scientific method (observation, hypothesis, prediction, and validation) to develop a general theory of recovery from which consistent application principles can be derived and used. That is not to say that successful recoveries have not been accomplished; they have. There have also been some notable failures. The distinguishing principles are not clear. What follows, then, are some predictable commonalities.

Organizing around the functions that you are almost certain to use is logical. Those are

- ➤ A direct connection to the company's policy-level executives

- ➤ A Recovery Team manager

- ➤ Clear assignment of the Recovery Team's functional responsibilities to individuals, some of whom may absorb more than one function

- ➤ Liaison with those responsible for restoration, or the short-term recovery function

- ➤ Information collection, evaluation, analysis, and dissemination

- ➤ Preliminary planning

- ➤ Liaison with stakeholders

- ➤ Financial aspects, including investigating potential grants, loans, insurance payments, and income generation to finance recovery

- ➤ Liaison with regulators, including government approval processes

➤ Ongoing management evaluation (what's working?)[9]

➤ Public relations

➤ Administrative support for those functions

■ THINKING OUTSIDE OF THE BOX

During long-term recovery, conditions are favorable to achieve a number of things that are unlikely during "business as usual." The Recovery Team can become an incubator that will identify and develop a company's future leaders because relatively junior managers can propose, develop, and implement miniprojects.

Here, too, are opportunities to mitigate a company's exposures to threats that have been present long enough to be thought of as part of the background noise. Along with mitigating longstanding threats, opportunities surface to make changes that acknowledge and reduce exposures to the recently changed terrorism strategies cited earlier as well as other threats that have increased either in frequency (shortened time between events) or in intensity (e.g., weather phenomena).

Unobtrusive architectural modifications can be made to make sites less attractive to terrorists and more common criminals. Examples are architectural lighting added or modified to enhance security, entries with sensor provisions built in, landscaping that includes large planters placed to improve vehicle standoff distances, automatic air-intake shutoffs installed to exclude smoke and chemicals, systems redundancy to eliminate single points of failure, and surveys to determine the potential for collateral damage from nearby occupancies (because they are likely terrorists' targets or because they generate their own hazards).

■ RECOVERY BY ATTEMPTED CONSENSUS

Where recovery includes substantial rebuilding or relocation—even partial relocation—dealing with local government becomes a factor. Local governments discover that
they in turn must deal with other stakeholders, who include
single-interest groups—sometimes very small groups who
learn to use the media to advance their agenda, which they
will attempt to tie to the relocation.

One can anticipate the appearances of single-interest
groups' representatives at public hearings, in letters to the
editor, and in interviews by getting the company's public relations staff to either research or employ a local media consultant. Failing that, a visit to local reporters who cover the
relocation area will usually identify the individuals and
their agendas. From there, it's Debating 101: Gather information to learn their strategy and help your company's public relations staff prepare facts and consider approaches to
gain support for the relocation, remembering that what is
merely relocation for your company represents change that
will concern the people where you are going. At this point,
readers who have not been through such events might be
wondering whether this is a real issue.

Governments recognize the ability of single-interest
groups to form effective coalitions for mutual support and
get attention for their agendas when an issue can be used. If
their agendas do not get the attention they seek, they become critics; elected officials become former elected officials; and their staffs discover the need to relocate. In
addition to the examples in Chapter 1, here are examples of
interest groups whose agendas got action.

The Loma Prieta earthquake demolished several buildings in the downtown business district of Santa Cruz and

rendered many more unsafe. Aside from that obvious destruction, the infrastructure was destroyed in several key places, which made substantial rebuilding necessary. A committee was appointed with several single-interest groups represented. Three years later, the rebuilding plan was accepted. Consensus had been difficult in part because resolving the problem of homelessness became part of the requirements.

The Oakland Hills fire resulted in much more than its obvious destruction. Fields of white ash between foundations showing occasional scrap-metal vestiges of furnishings offered no hope of anything left alive, and a police cordon kept all but the area's former residents out. However, the region's animal advocates gained the right to enter the exclusion zone. Their efforts saved many animals where even hope seemed pointless.

My point is that political realities are every bit as factual as physical realities. Readers who will have to deal with local politics to rebuild or relocate can facilitate the process by making the effort to learn the new local issues and adopt the interest groups' methods (except one): Seek alliances and be willing to compromise (but do not try direct opposition in their neighborhood).

One strategy for addressing those political realities with positive elements when recovery includes relocation or rebuilding is currently coming into favor and appears in enough written material to remain in the lexicon for some time. It is rebuilding or repositioning operations to be *sustainable*. *Sustainable* includes these attributes: resilience in the face of disruptive events; either enhancing, or at least not impacting, environmental quality; contributing to the local population's quality of life; enhancing the economic vitality of the local area; and playing a part in social equity.

The first and third items will probably be on your company's rebuild-relocate agenda, in any case.

Many in today's management environment are considering obtaining an advanced degree. Up to now, sustainability has been associated almost exclusively with governmental actions, but its relationship to the private sector — especially with companies' recovery actions after disruptive events — has been not much studied. Managers with responsibilities that include avoiding disasters who are considering advanced degrees could make real contributions to both fields by addressing sustainability as part of long-term, or strategic, recoveries. One resource is the University of Colorado Natural Hazards Center's project titled "Developing Guidance and Expertise on Sustainable Recovery from Disaster."[10]

On September 11 some of the terrorism rules did get rewritten — but the rules for recovery have always been different.

Chapter 8

They Can Help You, or ...

■ GOVERNMENT AND THE PRIVATE SECTOR: RULES OF ENGAGEMENT

We must all work together. That was true long before September 11, 2001, which only emphasized the truth that our society's public sector (government) and the private sector (business) must work together to stop disruptive events from entering the graveyard spiral that leads to catastrophes.

When thinking about the phases of emergency and crisis management, which have been the generally accepted starting point for studying and training to avoid disasters for at least the last 20 years, there is no phase that does not require cooperation and coordination between the public and private sectors for efficiency.

This is a chapter to help company managers who are responsible for planning and training to avoid disasters deal with their government counterparts. It will point out the commonalities, some of the acknowledged differences, and the unspoken differences that make coordination and cooperation both a necessity and a challenge. In this chapter there are also some training opportunities with government agencies that can benefit disaster avoidance program managers.

■ DUELING VIEWPOINTS CHALLENGE DISASTER AVOIDANCE MANAGERS

Most of us accept as a matter of course that a business is required and structured to produce revenue — enough revenue to cover all its costs and still return a profit — and that it should be managed to try to keep its profits greater than those of its competitors. That concept escapes most people who work in government.

It is not that they cannot intellectually grasp it or recognize that government and business must coexist in the same communities, but very few truly understand that it is necessary for businesses to thrive so that government can function well and the community's quality of life can bloom alongside both. Almost no local-government decision makers think about that when they are making the day-to-day decisions of their jobs. At the same time, few people in the private sector believe that the government can perform many functions as well as a business could, often viewing government with the feeling that it grasps more power than it is entitled to, wastes the resources entrusted to it, and increasingly endows itself with more regulatory powers that border on harassment of businesses.

Many senior managers believe that the less contact their companies have with government, the better. Those viewpoints put the manager who would assemble an efficient organization to thwart disasters in a challenging situation. Even so, public-private coordination and cooperation can be done; indeed, it *has* been done in the face of major disruptive events, and joint public-private systems have been preestablished by people recognizing that such events were surely approaching.

■ COMMONALITIES

Probably the public-private coordination familiar to most people is when local fire departments and their counterparts from refineries and other chemical processing companies join forces. In my experience, joint planning and training have been credited with reducing losses and concluding events sooner than otherwise would have happened. The need for coordination and compatible training continues to be important as one looks up the line of authority from field response to management.

During one event that threatened to turn into a large uncontrolled chemical reaction and send a cloud of hazardous materials into a large district of homes, three fire chiefs—two from nearby private sector refineries and one from the surrounding governmental fire district—used one of the refineries' Emergency Operations Centers to plan and stop the event. They combined both public and private resources in a strategy that eliminated the impending disaster. The fact that all were members of a public-private professional association and were aware of the available resources, including the companies' chemical experts, is an example of cooperation and coordination at management levels with a payoff in a crisis.

Another commonality is when senior management or executive-level policy backing is needed for disaster avoidance programs, which usually occurs at budgeting time. The city of Milpitas California long ago formed Business Partners for Emergency Preparedness, a group of corporations teamed with the city. All the members recognize their exposures in a part of California that can generate a number of serious disruptive events, including earthquakes strong enough to cause hazardous materials spills and fires simultaneously. Couple those with structural damage to buildings and disruption of the region's infrastructure to see why Business Partners for Emergency Preparedness members feel that their organization is vital. One of its great strengths is its ability to point out the investments of highly respected corporations with their dependence on the community's (in this case the fire department's Office of Emergency Services) support, and their availability to support their community's governmental emergency preparedness in turn.[1]

The previous chapter noted that committees, commissions, and other stakeholder groups are formed as adjuncts to the community's government after (and sometimes even before) disasters. It is worth reiterating here that corporate representation on those civic bodies is an excellent way both to keep informed about proposed mitigation activities and other issues that are likely to affect one's company and to make a significant and highly visible contribution to the community beyond the direct economic effects of just being there.

Some issues for public-private coordination that have surfaced in past events and preparedness seminars — and therefore might be something you would want in your notes as you conduct preplanning discussions with local government — follow:

➤ *Access during emergencies.* Businesses almost always want to get into their premises to get their vital records out, to do damage assessment, and to insure security. One organization thought that they had this issue managed until the local police invoked mutual aid for a large event. The highway patrol became the traffic control point's custodian but knew nothing of prior agreements with the police. One approach is ID cards that can be recognized by all law enforcement agencies of a region.

➤ *Infrastructure restoration.* Even other government agencies have trouble with this one. What is the priority for getting one's utilities restored? Who controls that? There may not be much your company can do to change its position in the sequence, but it is better to know in advance in order to begin planning for the darkness.

➤ *Emergency generators.* (1) Companies that provide generators have some that are *very* quiet. Local government's decision makers probably have not heard. (2) They need not be bolted down or in highly visible places. An outside plug-in will work (rental companies have them on roadworthy chassis). Can you get an agreement to get one through traffic control and parked for the duration where well-planned landscaping renders it invisible? (3) Local fire codes may not differentiate between emergency generator fuel and other flammable liquid or gas storage—not until your company opens the discussion, anyway.

➤ *Training.* (1) Local fire and rescue services like the visibility that comes with helping to train companies' Emergency Response Teams. Often, live (pan) fire extinguisher training and CPR are *very* low cost and provide excellent contacts before real events. (2) Local police services like the visibility that comes with training in their areas of expertise. Bomb-threats-through-detonation realities and self-protection against intentional workplace violence are examples. Ditto inexpensive, and ditto the excellent contacts previously noted.

➤ *Avoiding trouble before it arrives, 1:* Local governments' Fire Marshals and often the nearest engine company will conduct no-cost life and electrical

safety inspections. Their recommendations are seldom written, are almost always based on their real-
world experiences, and are easy to implement.

➤ *Avoiding trouble, 2:* Local police agencies will share local crime statistics and trends while offering ways to
divert muggers, graffiti vandals, and wanna-be bur-
glars elsewhere. They usually leave employee briefings to the company and point out where adding or
brightening a light or trimming foliage will be an inexpensive investment. Criminals fear light and unob-
structed sight lines.

➤ *Evacuations and relocations.* Most public health departments have specialists who provide services for
disabled people. Their advice could reduce liability
exposures at no cost and prevent a loss of public and
employee confidence.

■ DIFFERENCES

With some commonalities just identified, it is also true that
differences between the public and private sectors surface.
One of them is that in governmental agencies there are numerous detailed rules, which must be adhered to before
progress can be made. In short, government agencies are
often process driven. This is especially true when something unusual is being purchased beyond routine supplies
and services. In an attempt to minimize the influence of
salespeople who solicit project personnel, rules often for-
bid contact beyond a status check once the specifications
have been given to a purchasing officer to be contracted
out. Although a number of large corporate organizations
exhibit milder versions of being process driven, especially

at lower levels, businesses in general tend to be more focused on steps forward. In short, companies are more objective driven.

What businesspeople often miss in dealing with government employees is that the detailed rules slowing progress are equally frustrating to the people in the government agencies. This idea is discussed more in Chapter 10.

A second difference between government's management situation and that for businesspeople is time. Whereas government employees often determine early in a project's lifetime whether it is funded by *carryover money* (meaning that the budgetary appropriation can be used in a succeeding year or years), businesspeople are usually given an objective coupled to a fixed date.

In fairness to the governmental process, project slack time is sometimes built in because funding from elected officials may become sporadic, and sometimes only part of the total funds necessary for a project's completion is appropriated. Nonetheless, this can become a source of friction because the government's part of a project is not under a compelling sense of urgency, whereas the government employee's company counterpart watches a deadline inexorably approach—and with it a dreaded interview with his or her boss.

■ UNSPOKEN DIFFERENCES

One of the things that company managers working with their counterparts in governmental agencies should prepare for is that governmental managers work with considerably less funding—both in their personal compensation and for project funding—than the business's project manager has. For example, very few government agencies' senior managers have signature authority for significant amounts.

Their corporate counterparts can often direct appreciable funds with little need to obtain authorization before each purchase. Government agencies seldom have a line item in their budgets for charitable or public relations contributions, whereas most corporations do. This often leads to an unspoken discovery by government managers that their private sector colleagues have resources that they might put to use in the service of the public.

In one instance, the public safety agencies in a county had discovered multiple-casualty events and were struggling to coordinate the numerous agencies from several jurisdictions necessary to control those scenes and manage (especially the medical) response and transport casualties to the specialized care facilities matching their injuries. Although the issues were cloaked in the professional terminology of "mortality" and "morbidity" statistics, as well as "contributing factors," the responders understood that they were really talking about human lives lost or saved, how well the survivors could live the rest of their lifetimes, and how to prevent recurrences.

In that county a large refinery was preparing to phase out a block of portable radios as part of an overall upgrade for its communications. The refinery donated the radios to the county for use as a low-power, scene-of-action intercommunications system. The refinery's general manager had signature authority for the salvage value of those radios, and he was in the midst of an effort to convince the local community that his refinery is a responsible neighbor—and the scene control problem went away.

Without mutual representation on a joint public-private committee, neither refinery nor government representatives would likely have recognized the potential for that life-saving match and subsequent gift. When a tragic industrial accident occurred at that refinery, the interpersonal relationships between the government and corporate managers facilitated the information flows that made an efficient response.

In another instance of benefits from public-private interaction, a major natural hazard became a natural disaster. The government's regional coordinating agency was understaffed, and a private sector manager had an advanced degree that matched one of the needed positions. For several days his company made him available pro bono publico to fill that position as he selected additional staff to take that Emergency Operations Center into 24-7 operations, transition from manual to computerized operations, help develop the After Action Report, and later respond to audits.

The unspoken (and at first poorly understood) differences in those instances were signature authority coupled with the need for favorable publicity, as well as the flexibility to assign management personnel instantly. The private sector has them, and the public sector usually does not.

■ PUBLIC-PRIVATE RELATIONSHIP DEVELOPMENT

Because of the usual relationship between government-as-regulator and company-as-regulated, there are stages of development before regular public-private coordination and cooperation are achieved.

Governmental managers who are likely to be called to events at sites such as refineries should be forgiven if they are thinking, "What do you suppose they're up to behind that fence; is it going to impact us?" At the same time, managers on the other side of the fence should be forgiven for thinking, "They'll be in here with their clipboards and sampling devices, looking to cite us and fine us again." That's a skeptic's view of the first stage.

The second stage usually occurs after an event in which both government and company responders discover that they could have gained control of the incident sooner or managed it more efficiently if they had understood each other's capabilities (and limitations) better. This often leads to joint training. At first, it is pretty rudimentary: "I'll show you mine if you show me yours (i.e., vehicles and equipment)." As the responders begin to see the advantages of mutual interaction during emergencies, however, managers discover one another's competencies, and mutual respect develops.

The third stage usually occurs when those who must manage field responses from both the public and private sectors develop mutual guidelines for foreseeable disruptive events, with the goal of stopping the graveyard spiral. At this point public sector managers realize that their private sector counterparts can access resources beyond what is already standing in the roadway—*and* will not mind sharing them.

In one instance, local fire departments were chronically short of the bottles of compressed air that firefighters must wear in the hostile breathing environments that are their working conditions. Fire apparatus was being summoned as mutual aid and spare bottles stripped from fire companies still in quarters so those at the scene could continue to operate safely. Two refineries pooled funds to purchase a joint-use cascade system that could be brought to the scene and refill bottles regardless of whose fire it was.

The fourth stage occurs after public and private emergency field response (and their supporting) managers develop that mutual respect. The readers will please recall the illustration of the chiefs who overcame the impending uncontrolled chemical reaction disaster by pooling their collective knowledge and resources.

The fifth stage arrives when public and private disaster avoidance managers begin joint planning for ways to pool resources and prevent disruptive events from escalating. This includes going so far as to conduct joint management training exercises that involve both management teams.

Joint planning and expenditures to mitigate the effects of recognized threats that can impact the community will be the sixth stage. The reader probably noted the future tense.

■ GOVERNMENT TRAINING FOR MANAGERS: A BRIEF HISTORY OF DEVELOPMENT

There are several government training institutions for emergency managers. The Federal Emergency Management Agency's Emergency Management Institute (EMI) at Emmitsburg, Maryland, leads those in the United States. EMI transitioned from instructing an almost exclusively civil-defense (war damage) management environment into events that were occurring in the real world: disruptive events caused when natural, human-caused, and accidental threats short of war became disasters. EMI draws students from all U.S. states and territories and sometimes has foreign visitors as students. The California Specialized Training Institute at San Luis Obispo is the training arm of the governor's Office of Emergency Services. It had a real-world orientation before EMI but draws its students from the more limited confines of that one state.

Both institutes train managers in *integrated emergency management*, in which the management silos (or stovepipes) isolating fire from police, from emergency medical services, from public works, and so on are recognized as impediments to efficient responses and are removed. Recently, those changes that seemed almost revolutionary when first introduced have been augmented by adding the concept that the initial decisions get made in the field, and an Emergency Management Center — at least in the first stages of disruptive events — provides *logistics support* for the people out there where the rubber meets the road. Another advancement points to more private sector training opportunities at government institutes; it is the addition of mitigation and recovery phases to the established response curriculum. A community's total recovery necessarily includes its economic recovery.

■ GOVERNMENT TRAINING: TO WELCOME OR NOT TO WELCOME COMPANIES' EMERGENCY MANAGERS?

Despite the growing recognition that joint public-private cooperation, coordination, and training are increasingly essential at every level from response, through management, to policy — a viewpoint emphatically reinforced on September 11, 2001 — the opportunities for joint training remain limited and in fact have been restricted until very recently.

At first, only private sector managers whose companies had infrastructure responsibilities (power, health care, banking, transportation, etc.) were welcomed at both the California Specialized Training Institute and EMI as part of the student body whose expenses were paid. Other private sector manager-students had to pay their own expenses plus fees (it was still a bargain, in my opinion).

Then, without much elaboration, that policy was effectively relaxed to include private sector managers who came as part of a group from a community or region sponsored by the state's emergency management agency. In some cases, when the training came to communities, more private sector managers simply appeared in classes. Now, more private sector managers are appearing in courses at EMI. Logically, extension to incorporate those managers who will be planning to restore the economic well-being of their communities can be expected to expand.

Perhaps one of the greatest benefits is the public-private cross-pollination and exchange of experiences that occur during informal moments at such training facilities.

■ TRAINING CAVEATS: PRIVATE AND PUBLIC OFFERINGS

Attendance at the seminars sponsored by the two main American publications for private sector disaster avoidance has been increasing — and phenomenally, it seems to those who recall the initial round tables. Many of the training sessions offered at those seminars are excellent. However, attendees can benefit from more courses with case studies and principles for successful public and private collaborations.

There are now 73 higher education programs around the world granting degrees in emergency management or closely related subjects, and most programs are still oriented to educating public sector managers. Apparently, the case for business managers and joint business-government curricula in disaster preparedness and avoidance is not yet well developed. For interested readers, the higher education programs break down into 18 associate degree programs, 20 bachelor's degree programs, and 35 graduate degree programs.[2]

■ OTHER COUNTRIES, OTHER ISSUES

For readers with facilities outside of Australia and the Americas, it might be well to understand that governments sometimes fear that "outside" organizations (e.g., corporations and nonprofits) will attempt to subvert their people. In those places cooperation and coordination are unlikely, even if the company is merely trying to care for its own employees and their families by seeing that they resume work as soon as is practical.

Chapter 9

Rules, Regulations, and Standards

■ PURPOSE

This chapter is intended to help managers who have been given the lead responsibility for helping their companies avoid disasters to discover the following:

- ➤ What the company is required to do

- ➤ What the company may choose to omit (at risk of later being blamed for negligence)

- ➤ What the company's officers and other managers should consider to protect company assets as part of due diligence

- ➤ A base for the departure into the next chapter

■ CIVICS REPRISED: WHAT TO EXPECT

The legislative process at its best responds to a disruptive event that has impacted a significant number of people by moving to protect them from a repetition. When completely eliminating the next event is not practical, legislation is crafted to reduce the impacts. Legislation is necessarily broadly written because the process involves compromise and because it is not possible to foresee every future threat accurately. Usually, writing something at the policy level in the present can only lessen impacts. Practically, the best laws are policies that authorize regulations.

Regulations in turn contemplate real-world implementations and are the result of still more compromises. They are usually shaped during meetings called so that those likely to be affected by regulation may be heard. The anticipated results are adaptations to facilitate implementation without losing the sense of the authorizing law.

While the two processes just described are pretty much top-down, the third is rule making, which is often initiated at lower levels — sometimes to abate a risk and its potential impacts, and sometimes to stave off the threat of more restrictive laws or regulations. One characteristic of rules is that they tend to be imposed by organizations that cannot impose criminal penalties. Another characteristic of rules is that over time they can become so widely accepted that they become standards. When standards are ignored without good reason, others are encouraged to seek redress in civil legal actions. A third characteristic is that meetings to let the impacted be heard during development of regulations may not be held as rules get adopted.

Some organizations without the ability to impose legal penalties write what they describe as standards — usually by a process of consensus similar to the way in which regulations are written and adopted. There are examples of all of the above in the following citations.

◼ APPLICABLE TO ALL U.S. COMPANIES: VERY BASIC

➤ Section 1910.38 of Part 29, Code of Federal Regulations, Occupational Safety and Health Administration

The day after September 11, 2001, a business reporter for the *Los Angeles Times* contacted me to discuss requirements for companies to prepare for major emergencies. An experienced manager had told her that there was no requirement to prepare, and she thought it wise to seek confirmation, as good reporters will. I was able to fax her a copy of Section 1910.38 of Part 29 of the Code of Federal Regulations of the Occupational Safety and Health Administration (OSHA). In this part of this chapter, it is abbreviated to its essential parts, with commentary. However, almost all of 1910.38 is included in Appendix A of this chapter.

Not being an attorney, or holding myself out as competent to offer legal advice, I offer these citations only for readers' own interpretations. I recommend seeking the counsel of an attorney experienced in labor law for more insight. Readers are encouraged to obtain and review the regulations as published by the Office of the Federal Register and available from local bookstores of the Government Printing Office.

➤ Employee Emergency Plans and Fire Prevention Plans

The title seems to make it pretty clear that employee life safety is the issue. It goes on to say that plans must be in writing unless there are 10 or fewer employees, but the employer must still explain the plan and what employees are expected to do. It begins by specifically mentioning "fire and other emergencies," but in the guidelines of the appendix, it expands to include other threats to be expected in particular workplaces,such as toxic chemical releases, hurricanes, tornadoes, blizzards, and floods.

It lists minimum elements: emergency escape procedures with route assignments, procedures when certain employees are required to remain (e.g., to shut down processes), accounting for everyone after evacuation, rescue and medical duties, how to report emergencies, and whom to contact for further information.

An alarm system is required, and it must have specific signals if it is used for other purposes. Types of evacuations to match specific emergencies must be in the plan. Before implementing the plan, training enough people to assist in safe and orderly evacuation is required. Training is also required when the plan is developed, when the employee's responsibilities change, and when the plan changes. Every new employee must be trained about the plan.

The use of floor plans or workplace maps should be included in the emergency action plan, and the guideline recommends color-coding routes, with explanations of rescue and first aid duties. Then it reiterates that it means all employees. Several types of evacuations are discussed, and a ratio of 1 warden per 20 employees to facilitate evacuation is suggested, with the recommendation that they be trained to assist the disabled, search for stragglers, and account for employees after evacuation. Employers are further advised to coordinate plans with other employers in multitenant buildings.

➤ States and Local Jurisdictions Also Regulate

Addenda to Uniform Building Codes and Uniform Fire Codes

I was surprised to learn that one city in a major metropolitan area had designated any building over three stories to be a high rise, adding special life safety and fire department accomodations. The reason it developed is that each city can add its own annex or other modifications to the Uniform Fire Code. Many companies' facilities managers have either a fair knowledge of what is required at their site or access to an expert. I recommend checking the states where your company has facilities to determine whether they have similar requirements. The fire codes in particular address life safety issues — and they are not the same, even among cities in the same state and region.

A notation about building codes will probably be useful here. Particularly in areas where destructive natural threats occur, such as earthquakes, hurricanes, tornadoes, and wet snow accumulating on flat roofs, there is a temptation to think that the existing code will ensure that the structure one's company occupies will permit it to resume business after the event is over. Here are some realities:

➤ Building codes are usually updated every two years with the lessons learned from recent major events. Thinking of how long ago your company moved in may approximate how many important changes have not been incorporated into the building.

➤ Building codes are written principally to protect the people inside. Although the building may not collapse on its occupants, it may never again be usable.

➤ Building codes require features that assume good workmanship. If corners were cut or if the workers did not appreciate that the code should be carefully followed, the building will not perform as expected. For example, when the walls are not bolted to the foundation about every 18 inches, a moderate earthquake can separate the building's frame from its foundation, dropping the building to the ground, destroying its structural integrity, or distorting the frame beyond repair (architects and engineers say "wracked").

➤ Additions sometimes ignore important parts of building codes or change the wind-resistant character of a building so that it no longer affords the protection originally designed into it. For example, adding a wing or extension may provide a way for high winds to destroy a building by lifting a corner or an eave, which then allows the roof to be peeled off, admitting the wind to an interior space (one hears, "The wind got under the roof and lifted it off, destroying the building's integrity, demolishing it room by room, and drenching its contents").

➤ When your company is contemplating construction, become involved to help avoid disaster. Note that building to existing code is the lowest standard permitted, and it may not incorporate lessons learned from recent destructive events.

➤ Where there is extensive glass to windward and potential missiles such as furniture, trash cans, and maintenance equipment, if these are not removed from the grounds before wind speeds increase, broken glass can admit wind and water, increasing the interior air pressure on the downwind windows, and so on, rendering the building codes moot.

Following are some important recommendations to disaster avoidance program managers: (1) With an expert advisor (not a building contractor) and the facility's manager, see what changes have been made to the building codes since the building went up and determine whether modifications can overcome deficiencies. (2) Review the experiences of others to discover what damages occurred to similar buildings during the kinds of events that happen where you are. (3) Add engineers authorized by the local buildings department to do quick postevent surveys to your plan's resources section. Also add board-up,[1] cleanup, and building contractors. (4) Determine whether local rules permit rebuilding to the former code instead of the current ones. (5) If rebuilds must match current code, determine with the risk manager if the casualty insurer will reimburse adequately.

■ APPLICABLE TO FINANCIAL INSTITUTIONS

> ## ➤ Office of the Comptroller of the Currency Bulletin 97-23: Corporate Business Resumption and Contingency Planning

Office of the Comptroller of the Currency (OCC) Bulletin 97-23 is a policy statement by the Federal Financial Institutions Examination Council (FFIEC), or bank examiners, on corporate business resumption and contingency planning. The essence of what is expected and how to approach it is in its four-page attachment, which says (paraphrased) the following:

> ➤ Its purpose is to alert the board of directors and management to the need for contingency planning, whether their institution does its own processing or uses a service bureau.

> ➤ Contingency planning establishes strategies to
> > ➤ Minimize service disruptions.
> > ➤ Minimize financial loss.
> > ➤ Ensure timely resumption of operations when a disaster occurs.

> ➤ Information technology now includes much more than central processing; therefore, "contingency planning now requires institution-wide emphasis," and "contingency planning by financial institution services is equally important" (emphasis in original).

➤ Concerns include the following:

  ➤ Many contingency plans do not address all critical functions throughout the institution.

  ➤ Many institutions have no contingency planning with their service bureaus.

  ➤ Many service bureaus have no contingency plans.

  ➤ Many plans have not been adequately tested.

➤ Regarding policy, the board of directors and senior management are responsible for the following:

  ➤ Establishing policies, procedures, and responsibilities for comprehensive contingency planning.

  ➤ Reviewing and approving the plans annually, documented in board minutes.

  ➤ Evaluating the plans of its service bureau.

  ➤ Ensuring that their plan is compatible with their service bureau's.

Following the attachment is an appendix with an example process for developing contingency plans, which bears a strong resemblance to the steps described in Chapters 2 and 3 of this book, plus some items specific to financial institutions.

Most large financial institutions have committed appreciable resources to their electronic data processing and information systems (IS) readiness and therefore readily pass FFIEC examinations of their electronic data processing and IS departments. However, many such institutions believe that their institution-wide readiness is not given equal weight in those examinations and thus have not achieved a comparable degree of readiness in the business units that are the IS department's internal customers.

OCC Bulletin 97-23 is reproduced in Appendix B of this chapter for readers who would like to review it in its entirety.

Readers are encouraged to obtain the most recent revision from the FFIEC at 1776 G Street, NW, Suite 701, Washington, DC, 20006, or by phoning (202) 874-2340 or downloading it from www.occ.treas.gov/OCC_current.htm.

■ APPLICABLE TO PUBLIC OR PRIVATE ORGANIZATIONS RESPONDING TO HAZARDOUS MATERIALS SPILLS

➤ **Part 29, Code of Federal Regulations, Section 1910.120**

If your employees respond to hazardous materials releases (called hazardous *substance* releases in this part of the OSHA Labor Code), section 1910.120, beginning at (q), is important for your planning. It addresses the emergency response plan and describes its elements in some detail. Notable requirements are planning and coordination with outside parties, training and levels of training, decontamination, postevent critiques with follow-ups, handling the response using the incident command system with a required staff safety person, support, requirements for medical baseline data with subsequent monitoring, and protective clothing. It, too, is downloadable, at www.OSHA.gov/SLTC/emergency response/index.html, or obtainable in book form from the Government Printing Office's bookstores.

■ APPLICABLE TO PUBLIC AND PRIVATE ORGANIZATIONS WITH EMERGENCY MANAGEMENT OR BUSINESS CONTINUITY PROGRAMS

➤ **National Fire Protection Association Standard 1600**

The National Fire Protection Association (NFPA) notes on the cover of this standard that it is an international codes and standards organization. It develops its documents by selecting a committee of qualified individuals representing various elements with an interest in the document's topic or with interests in using it as a standard, and then works for consensus. The process in this case took approximately 10 years, but in general, NFPA's process produces good results. I believe that this is such an example of a case where the drawn-out process produced a usable standard with requirements that can save lives and businesses. I also believe that managers should not think that NFPA 1600 applies only to developing disaster response plans for organizations that are principally fire oriented.

There are some issues around using a copyrighted document, which NFPA addresses through licensing. I have reviewed NFPA 1600 and consider it comprehensive, with an adequate framework on which to build a program.

The document is available from National Fire Protection Association, 1 Batterymarch Park, PO Box 9101, Quincy, MA, 02269-9101; by phone at (800) 344-3555; or on line at www .NFPA.org/Home/index.asp (click on codes and standards).

■ APPLICABLE TO HEALTH CARE ORGANIZATIONS

➤ Joint Commission on Accreditation of Healthcare Organizations Standard E. § c.1.4: Emergency Management

With revisions effective January 2001, this standard represents recent changes in both the detail and the implementation of assessing the readiness of health care institutions. They must be ready either to manage a disruptive event on their own premises or to prepare to receive casualties from a disaster in their catchment area.

The changes in detail are largely the incorporation of lessons learned from major disruptive events and the adoption of principles that have become generally accepted among business continuity professionals in recent years. This is no longer the last generation's hospital disaster checklist. Requirements now include a self-evaluation vulnerability (risk) analysis, specifics for interoperability with the community that the institution serves, identification of staff, support for personnel (housing, transport, critical incident stress debriefing, family support), recognition of potential vertical *or* horizontal evacuations, and security and media issues, among others.

The change in readiness assessments include random inquiries of the facility's staff during accreditation evaluations to determine how much employees know about the facility's overall disaster plan and about their specific roles and assignments. Data from the emergency management part of the overall evaluation are now given equal weight with the other parts, and revisits are scheduled when the evaluations are less than good.

E. § c.1.4 is downloadable from www.jcaho.org/standard/ ecer.html or can be ordered from the Joint Commission on Accreditation of Healthcare Organizations, 1 Renaissance Boulevard, Oakbrook Terrace, IL, 60181; phone, (630) 792-5000; fax, (630) 792-5005.

APPENDIX A: SECTION 1910.38 OF PART 29, CODE OF FEDERAL REGULATIONS, OCCUPATIONAL SAFETY AND HEALTH ADMINISTRATION, AND ITS APPENDIX.

➤ **§ 1910.38 Employee emergency plans and fire prevention plans.**

(a) Emergency action plan —

(1) Scope and application. This paragraph (a) applies to all emergency action plans required by a particular OSHA standard. The emergency action plan shall be in writing (except . . . [2]) and shall cover those designated actions employers and employees must take to ensure employee safety from fire and other emergencies.

(2) Elements. The following elements, at a minimum, shall be included in the plan:

(i) Emergency escape procedures and emergency escape route assignments;

(ii) Procedures to be followed by employees who remain to operate critical plant operations before they evacuate;

(iii) Procedures to account for all employees after emergency evacuation has been completed;

(iv) Rescue and medical duties for those employees who are to perform them;

(v) The preferred means of reporting fires and other emergencies; and

(vi) Names and job titles of persons or departments who can be contacted for further information or explanation of duties under the plan.

(3) Alarm system.[3]

(i) The employer shall establish an employee alarm system that complies with § 1910.165.

(ii) If the employee alarm system is used for alerting fire brigade members, or for other purposes, a distinctive signal for each purpose shall be used.

(4) Evacuation. The employer shall establish in the emergency action plan the types of evacuation to be used in emergency circumstances.

(5) Training.

(i) Before implementing the emergency action plan, the employer shall designate and train a sufficient number of persons to assist in the safe and orderly evacuation of employees.

(ii) The employer shall review the plan with each employee covered by the plan at the following times:

(A) Initially when the plan is developed,
(B) Whenever the employee's responsibilities or designated actions under the plan change, and
(C) Whenever the plan is changed.

(iii) The employer shall review with each employee upon initial assignment those parts of the plan that the employee must know to protect the employee in the event of an emergency. The written plan shall be kept at the workplace and made available for employee review.[4]

➤ Appendix

§ 1910.38 *Employee emergency plans.*

1. *Emergency action plan elements.* The emergency action plan should address emergencies that the employer may reasonably expect in the workplace. Examples are: fire; toxic chemical releases; hurricanes; tornadoes; blizzards; floods; and others. The elements of the emergency action plan presented in paragraph 1910.38(a)(2) can be supplemented by the following to more effectively achieve employee safety and health in an emergency. The employer should list in detail the procedures to be taken by those employees who have been selected to remain behind to care for essential plant operations . . . [Examples are provided]

The use of floor plans or workplace maps which clearly show the emergency escape routes should be included in the emergency action plan. Color coding [is recommended].

The employer should also develop and explain in detail what rescue and medical first aid duties are to be performed and by whom. All employees are to be told what actions they are to take in these emergency situations that the employer anticipates may occur in the workplace.

2. *Emergency evacuation.* At the time of an emergency, employees should know what type of evacuation is necessary and what their role is in carrying out the plan. In some cases where the emergency is very grave, total and immediate evacuation of all employees is necessary. [Delayed and local evacuations and relocations are described]

The designation of refuge or safe areas for evacuation should be determined and identified in the plan. [Divided buildings are described; using exterior refuge or safe areas is advocated; examples are given.]

3. *Emergency action plan training.* [The training is required, and this guideline recommends a ratio of 1 warden per 20 employees. It discusses the training that they should receive, including assisting handicapped employees, checking for stragglers, and accounting for employees after evacuation. Employers are advised to coordinate plans with other employers in multitenant buildings.]

Appendix B: Office of the Comptroller of the Currency Bulletin 97-23: Federal Financial Institutions Examination Council Interagency Statement on Corporate Business Resumption and Contingency Planning

TO: Chief Executive Officers of all National Banks, Department and Division Heads, and all examining personnel.

On March 26, 1997, the Federal Financial Institutions Examination Council adopted the revised policy statement (SP-5) Corporate Business Resumption and Contingency Planning. The statement continues to emphasize the importance of a business recovery and explains the goals associated with an effective business resumption and contingency plan. Revisions to this statement acknowledge the increased use of distributed computer environments and increased reliance on external service providers for mission-critical bank activities. The board of directors and senior management are urged to consider these distributed computer platforms and outsourced functions when conducting business resumption and contingency planning activities.

The revision was conducted as part of the combined agency Community Development and Regulatory Improvement Act (CDRIA) effort. Section 303 of CDRIA requires that the federal bank and thrift regulatory agencies review and streamline their regulations and written policies in order to improve efficiency; reduce unnecessary cost; eliminate unwarranted constraints on credit availability; and remove inconsistent, outmoded, and duplicative requirements.

For further information, contact Norine A. Richards, national bank examiner, Bank Technology Unit (202) 874-2340.

James Kamihachi
Senior Deputy Comptroller,
Economic and Policy Analysis

Chapter 10

FAQs ... and Common Sense

Welcome to the advanced course! This chapter is for those reader-managers who have absorbed the previous nine chapters, and perhaps sneaked a peek at Chapter 10, and are thinking, "OK, I've got it so far—but has the author got some more to take me a bit farther?" Or perhaps someone with a lot of experience picked up this book, and is thinking, "Will he share with us some of the really fine points picked up over those years?" The answers are "Yes!" and "Yes!!"

Will this chapter cover it *all*, right up to the minute? Not possible. Why not? The several fields of knowledge that comprise this profession are moving too fast. As I was browsing the Internet before sending the manuscript off to the publisher—just to be sure there were no late-breaking developments this book should include—the issues seen waiting in the wings for discussion next week were striking in their potentials for change. Certainly, the follow-on events stemming from September 11, 2001, had not yet settled onto their cruising courses by April 2002. What you have in your hands in an honest attempt to put the essentials onto the desks of managers who want to avoid disasters, with enough information to point the way for their own explorations once they have gotten most of this.

How to get there from here? No manager could do better than to join the closest professional association and to be a consistent attendee. The *Disaster Recovery Journal* (www.drj.com) lists most of those in the United States, and the next chapter gives additional offshore contacts. The next step is to become certified, and Chapters 2 and 4 opened the discussion about which certifications provide the best matches for readers' situations. But what if a reader would like to explore that further, or get beyond that? I am always honored and pleased when a colleague—of whatever experience level—calls or e-mails to exchange ideas or news. Please feel free to do that (buscontin@aol.com).

Like most FAQs, this chapter uses my own thoughts about what those might be because the reader is not yet in place to deliver those questions. Let us hope the guesswork is not far off.

Chapter 1 raised the specter that a disruptive event could enter what pilots call a graveyard spiral, becoming a crisis, then a disaster, and then a catastrophe—meaning that the corporation's continued existence could be put at risk. Just in case there were doubters, or those with short memories, some examples were produced. Arthur Andersen has struggled to overcome the lost confidence that followed Enron and to avoid breakup. As of this writing, it is doubtful that Andersen will survive in anything like the form it had pre-Enron. Releasing 70 percent of its partners will almost guarantee that—no matter what the outcome of the criminal trial is.

The Andersen example brings out a significant point that readers may want to ponder and share with their bosses. The techniques for avoiding disaster in an event like a hurricane are not much different than from a storm or repercussions with any other etiology.

Even if you choose not to hold that discussion with your boss, do not miss that point. Readers who think ahead and develop the skills of mustering and directing the expertise necessary to work through a crisis brought on by terrorists are developing the vision and leadership that corporations (and the rest of the world) desperately need for all other crises. Readers should not be shy about getting that onto their resumes and making sure that it surfaces in interviews and networking conversations. People who can prepare for and manage crises are valuable resources with unique skills. Is the reader thinking, "In a crisis, people somehow rise to the occasion"? Yes, they do—those who knew it was coming and practiced so that they would be ready. I give you Rick Rescorla, of Morgan Stanley, and Chapter 8.

Something else might have gone by one or two readers. Government emergency managers might think, because most of the metaphors in this book use "corporation" and such words, that the principles do not match their needs. Please go over the material again, and think of the many parallels that government managers have with those in the private and not-for-profit sectors. Translation ought to be virtually instantaneous for experienced managers.

The cascades of misfortunes in Chapter 1's illustrations are by no means unique. Readers who know some of the illustrations in James Gleick's book *Chaos Theory: Making a New Science* will recall the butterfly that started a hurricane. Conditions really *do* have periods of instability—ask any stock broker! Companies and governments that do not establish a system to stop the sequence leading to ruin are ignoring the lessons of history—or making the fool's bet that "it probably won't happen on *my* watch."

Anyway, it is not about casualties, destruction, financial losses, or shutdown functions. Think of the anthrax scare. Or

Three Mile Island. Or the next time you stand in those lines for airport security.

It is about lost confidence.

Chapter 1 laid the basis for Chapter 2, which presented the first half of the 10 steps that have become standard for developing a disaster avoidance (or business continuity or disaster recovery — depending on your background) program. So Chapter 2 was titled "Basic Stuff," which is pretty much what it is. Why break the 10 steps into two sections of 5? *Span of control.* One of the basic rules of crisis management (and cockpit management during in-flight emergencies) is to keep the number of rapidly changing variables down to something manageable. I can only imagine how many Stephen Hawking can handle, but for most of us, the magic number is around five.

Anyway, it is not about feeding information to the reader as if he or she were a child. It is about putting tools into the reader's hands that he or she can use in developing a program to avoid disaster. Taking it five or so points at a time is a basic presentation skill. Clank! Another tool in the tool bag.

A few things from Chapter 2 are worth emphasizing here. Choose the goal carefully. Hedge a bit by keeping it vague enough, and keep the objectives "for sure" do-able. Better to run ahead slowly than to become overconfident and risk that loss of confidence. Another bit of wisdom that I have gained along with numerous gray hairs and areas of scar tissue is to *avoid unsponsored projects.* I once suggested to a client's inside manager that it was time for some publicity; after all, the project was perking along, and he had made some very good things happen toward protecting the company against disruptive events. He was horrified. Unknown to me until that moment, he had been moving bits of funding from other accounts into the one for which there was no board-approved line item — avoiding disasters!

Not just a sponsor. A *champion*! And, like all conscientious professionals who would avoid disaster, look for a backup.

Shortly after my shock at learning that our good work was based on a bootleg budget, the same client's director of information services announced that the company would be consolidating its three data processing centers in the name of efficiency, and over his dead body. One basket, three fragile eggs. How fragile? How many companies will not recover from September 11? If the word-of-mouth data can be used as a guide, between 35% and 50% will crumble.

Chapter 2 let two cats out of the bag, big time. The secrets are out. Cat 1: The reason for the quantifiable risk analysis is really to get some pretty subjective scenarios. Why? Because that will bring the implementers—the critical unit managers—aboard the project. They will understand their contributions to profitability are on the line. Cat 2: It really isn't about the plan, although that *is* a necessary intermediate step, not to be abandoned, even later. What it is really about is getting to have a trained and rehearsed Crisis Management Team. Once its members are familiar with their roles and how to play together, the type of crisis (e.g., Arthur Andersen, Tora Bora) does not really matter to them. Think of a lion pride when a fat new herbivore steps onto their veldt for the first time. If they know what they are doing, they will recognize the threat, all right. More protein.

Please do not believe the three Appendixes of Chapter 2 uncritically. They are there to provide you with basic frameworks you can adapt to your own corporate culture and surroundings.

Chapter 3's slightly menacing title was meant to evoke both good and bad recollections. The "Prisoner of the Rose Garden" may have had something in common with a current statehouse incumbent who inherited an essentially unplanned deregulation crisis. Neither situation got better because neither official has the manage-by-delegating tool in his toolbox (insert the absence of a clank here). With the need for decisions coming well above almost anyone's comfort level, the Crisis Management Team's manager can send (indeed, *should* send) most decisions down to his or her tier of functional managers—as long as the span of control does not get too broad. *And* there are certain decisions that should go up to senior management along with the integrated analysis of options. As one of the admirals said during a recent Pentagon news conference, "*That* one is above my pay grade." The media had to wait for the answer to that one, but they all laughed.

There is, however, a practical risk that readers should watch for while conducting Crisis Management Team training exercises. The team should self-limit kicking decisions upstairs to the two suggested categories to avoid the somewhat natural tendency for middle managers to kick too many upstairs in a crisis. This brings us to the other side of that coin: senior management's natural tendency to take over too many decisions from middle management. Senior managers who climbed the corporate ladder, American-style, can revert under stress.

Until recently, the term *hot site* described those places providing computers to which companies that lose the use of their usual computing base can retreat, but that term became associated mainly with an already-running, in-place computer. Now that the accepted—and for financial institutions, mandated[1]—practice holds that *all* business units should be included in business continuity planning, *alternate work site* is a better term that more closely represents the inclusive approach.

About getting the best awareness of the disaster avoidance program: Training programs, through the informal communications webs (grapevines) existing in all organizations, will create awareness as soon as the team recruiting, selection, and training sequence starts. If the recruitment, selection, and training processes create an aura that Emergency Response Team members, Emergency Medical Technicians, and Crisis Management Team members are elite cadres with special responsibilities and recognition, the positive buzz will increase further.

A word to the wise readers from an experienced person: For heaven's sake, *pilot* the training using publicity shots for recruiting and program awareness while the wise program manager debugs the pilot training, making it ready for full-scale deployment.

Some practical points about exercises match those about program kickoffs. Keep an exercise's goal under control—not too ambitious at first—until the manager knows what objectives are practical. One is always to minimize disrupting the company's ongoing profitable work. A second point is safety when directing field forces (Emergency Response Teams). That leaves three, if the reader remembers and agrees that more than five things are hard for most people to keep simultaneously in mind.

To push a little harder on that safety topic: For full-scale (field) exercises, one of the objectives should be a safety statement, making clear to all participants that risk of injury is not acceptable. Keep the scenario subordinate to the training objectives, and keep it not just realistic but also believable to the participants. Remember that their experience is limited—they may not have even read this book.

One of the best ways to involve key implementers and foster their enthusiasm for developing the test is to include them in the Simulation Group. They can get involved in writing the initial messages and making actions conform to the training objectives.

When setting up exercises, remember that it takes a minimum of two people to maintain control: one controller in with the Crisis Management Team, and the other controller keeping the Simulation Group focused on the objectives. Once the test's objectives are achieved, avoid abrupt cutoffs that leave involved players in an emotional no-man's-land. Wind it down with messages that make the issues dissolve.

After exercises, keeping the Lessons Learned discussion constructive is easy if you begin by separating into disciplines or functional groups (logistics people meet with other logistics people, etc.) to have a wide topic-range debriefing. Let each group pick one spokesperson who cuts his or her group's list to the three things that the group believes the rest of the groups should hear. Be sure the spokespersons know that back in the plenary session there were no-fault rules. Directly criticizing another group or person is out. Those kinds of things should be captured on the Lessons Learned Lists that go directly to the exercise controller. Spokespersons should be sure to praise as well. In that way, players will leave with a positive state of mind and will be willing to participate in the follow-on training (and thank you, Niccolò Machiavelli).

Regarding the participation of senior management in training exercises, although senior managers' scheduling is intense, they often participate when discretely reminded how important their leadership is to managers coming up the line behind them. When the word gets around that a senior manager plans to attend, others are encouraged to become active in the planning and to attend the exercise. The potential for senior managers' positive visibility during a crisis when they have become familiar with the emergency management system before a disaster strikes can be (once again, discretely) emphasized.

A note for those who will be managing a series of exercises. It is logical to use the alternates for the Emergency Management Team's principals in the Simulation Group. This has additional benefits: First, a subordinate is unlikely to pile on too many problems and allow his or her boss to reach a high level of frustration; second, the subordinate as alternate receives some training early on in the process; third, depth in the team's roster can be achieved by moving the Simulation Group into the Crisis Management Center after a few exercises and asking the principals to become the Simulation Group. The bosses frequently respond to that suggestion with enthusiasm, as it provides opportunities for a gentle game of "what goes around comes around."

A note to managers contemplating that age-old issue, "Do I really want to go into full-scale exercises (with field teams and simulated casualties and damage)?": I recommend using combined Evaluator-Safety Monitors, carefully placed, with instructions to stop the exercise in their vicinity and correct any developing situation that threatens to result in injury or property damage. Training the Evaluator-Safety Monitors and briefing them before the exercise are essential, as is some means of identification that is obvious to all participants in the field. Participants should also be briefed to understand that an instruction about safety from an Evaluator-Safety Monitor is not a suggestion.

After every exercise, complete Lessons Learned Lists should be collected from the groups involved. Those lists will be too long for discussion at the review and analysis (never say "critique") session immediately following the exercise; therefore, each business unit involved should pick a spokesperson (as earlier). The manager responsible for emergency preparedness can then review the complete lists and prepare a report with recommendations for senior management.

When an organization's emergency preparedness program

is in its early stages, before the plan is much more than an outline, conducting a small functional exercise can have large benefits. Those who participate will provide a wealth of information as parts of their Lessons Learned Lists, and they will usually develop a desire to see the program do well because they become aware of potential impacts on their business units. Anyway, it is not about data gathering (another secret, here); exercises are *fun*. Preparing a draft report for the senior's signature and disseminating it among senior management can greatly accelerate implementation of the preparedness program.

At the beginning of each exercise after the initial table-top walkthrough, time for the Simulation Group's leader to brief the Simulation Group is necessary:

➤ Cover maintaining control while ensuring that the test's objectives are achieved.

➤ Cover keeping the Simulators' Lessons Learned constructive so that the other players also leave with a positive state of mind.

Chapter 3 also addressed some of the more important issues around public relations:

➤ Beware of compromising your spokesperson's credibility, which exists only with reporters who know him or her, anyway. Once that's gone, you will probably have to fire him or her.

➤ Make sure that your big kahuna is well briefed and rehearsed before he or she is trotted out, as will be inevitable if media attention gets strong enough, with subject-matter experts rehearsed and close at hand when the camera lights come on.

➤ Remember that the media are the public's window on the world, so everyone should know not to try to go off the record. Reporters do not keep two notebooks.

➤ Realize that no matter what a reporter may ask, you must get your company's vital messages out. Your company's largest audience, and therefore most of the public's (and the other stakeholders') impressions, will be locked into those moments when your spokespersons are speaking through the news medias' cameras.

Chapter 6 addressed redundant systems to meet a business continuity (Strategy 2) requirement. A key to getting redundancies approved is to have uses for them until they are put in service to defeat outages. A bonus to having them in continuous use, instead of standby, is that because they are operational, they are likely to be maintained, and people will know how to use them. Therefore, they will be available for immediate emergency use.

Also from Chapter 6: Entirely aside from direct financial costs, the lost confidence in certain industries (financial, health care, and anything moving at freeway speeds) will impose additional costs to which few brand managers would consent. The same is true of the increased costs that additional regulation brings in the wake of lost confidence. You see? It *is* about confidence.

There are additional impacts, which are listed and described in Appendix A of Chapter 4. The point for discussion when talking up the disaster avoidance program is that when selecting strategies, achieving a balance between direct financial costs and the benefits from reducing those impacts requires careful consideration and discussion with other managers who will have to deal with the specific types of impacts. That puts the business continuity or disaster avoidance director in the nearly unique position of seeing across the stovepipes and silos that isolate most managers within their divisions. The Crisis Management Team gets the same benefit, but the planner gets there sooner—good grooming for a policy-level position.

Chapter 7 discussed the next disruptive event drawing nearer all the time. The underlying reason for trying to accelerate improvements evoked from either real-world experiences (using other people's is OK) or exercise simulations is that that next disruptive event *is* drawing closer while changes are being negotiated. Some may consider that to be an overstatement, but there are plenty of authorities (please see a resources list of publications and Web sites in Chapter 11) that have the numbers. See also the Web sites for MunichRe (www.munichre.com) and the Federal Emergency Management Agency (FEMA; www.fema.gov). They draw us inescapably to know that disasters are becoming (1) more frequent with (2) increasing losses and (3) more people involved as the years pass. There are many reasons, and I leave it to the material published there to help readers make their case.

In Chapter 8 I said, "When thinking about the four phases of emergency and crisis management, which have been the generally accepted starting point for studying and training to avoid disasters for at least the last 20 years, there is no phase that does not require cooperation and coordination between the public and private sectors for efficiency." What's wrong with that statement? It doesn't go far enough.

I should point out the need to include the not-for-profit sector, which has problems beyond the apathy plaguing most of our public-private relationships. The not-for-profits that people see as charitable, well-motivated organizations are seen as competing for the populace's loyalty in many third world countries. This is valuable information for readers whose responsibilities will include corporate facilities in those countries. Corporate program managers who would like to provide self-help and family protection guidelines should beware of being tarred with the same brush that third-world governments would apply to the not-for-profits.

In governmental agencies there are numerous detailed rules that must be adhered to before progress can be made. I hope that this point got nailed down pretty well. However, in most agencies there is an experienced employee who knows the rules so well that he or she can tell one how to make progress occur without becoming completely frustrated by a host of rules that seem to be put there to block getting much accomplished. Find and cultivate that person because what businesspeople often miss in dealing with government employees is that the detailed rules slowing progress are equally frustrating to the government agencies' people. This can provide an opportunity to recognize common ground when coordinating with government employees to get something done.

When speaking of opportunities for joint training at government facilities, the point was made that some almost-revolutionary changes (to stop pointing at civil defense and ditch the stovepipes blocking interdepartmental communications) have been augmented by adding the concept that the initial decisions get made in the field, and thus that an Emergency Management Center has, at least at first, a *support* role for the people out there where the rubber meets the road. Yes, but . . .

Eventually, decisions about priorities come back into the Emergency Management Center because inevitably the situation deteriorates to one in which too many requirements are being pursued by too few resources. Implications: Set forth well-defined priorities and their rationales before someone has to apply priorities to scarce resources under pressure.

And so ends the advanced course, or hints and kinks for astute readers. I hope they were accepted in the spirit offered—that is, in the belief that there is no reason for readers to acquire the same scars that I picked up in the process of learning these things the hard way.

Readers will have many opportunities to acquire their own.

Chapter 11

Help beyond These Covers

■ ONE MORE THING TO DO FOR YOU, READER

This book was written to walk a manager new to business continuity and disaster avoidance through three years of learning in however little time it takes to get from cover to cover, then to be a desk reference whenever the manager needs to recall a concept, connect some thoughts, or rekindle an idea. That approach necessarily left some specialized areas unaddressed. In addition, change is certain; the only uncertainty is *how* change will occur. As approaches change and rules are rewritten, some things that were perfectly factual as they went into any book change after the book lands on the manager's desk.

This chapter is here at the book's end to provide readers with easy-to-find specialized areas, with points to monitor to check on how things are changing, and with a bibliography for readers who want to do more research.

■ SPECIALIZED AREAS

One constant in this business of avoiding disasters is change. It is not just that change is constant; it seems that the rate of change is accelerating. As we think about that phenomenon, it is logical: More people become involved at the management level, and our collective understanding of the issues reveals their real complexity. That's the good news, of course: Our understanding is growing. The challenge is to expand our personal resources quickly enough to stay adequately connected.

Just when we who have been working in the profession for a while begin to relax, thinking we have contacts for almost all items of specialized knowledge that are not in our own area of expertise, a new issue surfaces. So the chase is on again, with the question, "How quickly can we find out who has at least one of the keys to the newly surfaced issue?" Another piece of good news is that the great majority of professionals in this business are more than willing to share what they know—probably because we all know that reciprocity multiplies our personal databases of knowledge. One hears from time to time that a good manager is never more than three phone calls away from the answer.

So, at this point I will point out some places to call or browse for specialized expertise. No organization on these pages ever asked for an endorsement, so some may be a little surprised to be listed. Or some may be a little surprised if a reader calls using this reference. The reader shouldn't be surprised at that.

Building Code, Fire Code, and Life Safety Issues

The McMullen Company
(530) 757-1291
www.themcmullencompany.com

Casualty Management Planning

Olson and Associates
(925) 788-4473
j3cubolson@aol.com

Children in Disasters

E. A. Warren & Associates
(650) 201-8848
iwander@pacbell.net

Communications, Indoor Alerting

Emergency Management Group International
(530) 613-2289
joshemgi@quiknet.com

Communications, Outdoor Alerting

Procomm
(510) 352-9195
ProcommNCa@cs.com

Communications, Public Relations

Lexicon Corporation
(213) 346-1200
www.lexiconcorp.com

Communications, Putting It All Together

Incident Communications
(707) 425-4916
www.incident.com

Communications, Switching Reliability

Learnability
(925) 631-3790
jln@learnability.com

Crisis Management Plan Testing and Training

Tal Global
(408) 993-1300
www.talglobal.com

Crowds, Public Assembly Safety

GraCorp
(804) 304-4217
GraCorpPrz@aol.com

Emergency Response Teams

North American Emergency Management, Inc.
(415) 527-6482
fjlucier@naem.com

Energy Industry Issues

Business Continuity Services
(925) 260-5143
rjnebay@sprynet.com

Executive Education, Crisis Management

Comprehensive Crisis Management
(310) 374-0063
info@compcrisis.com

Institute for Crisis and Disaster Management
(202) 994-7153
harrald@seas.gwu.edu

Government Liaison, States

Challenging Hazards Applying Technology
(317) 542-1315
airborne@surf-ici.com

Government Liaison, U.S. Federal

Claire Rubin & Associates
(703) 920-7176
crubin@mindspring.com

Information Systems Design Strategic Issues

Swihart Group
(925) 829-2728
stanswi@earthlink.net

Information Systems Mitigation and Recovery

Vegavir Corporation
(408) 924-3569
www.vegavir.com

Public-Private Cooperation and Coordination

PrivatePublicPartnerships
(202) 721-1536
pripubpart@aol.com

Williams Associates
(925) 370-2295
oneclw@msn.com

Senior Management Assurances

Cole Emerson & Associates
(916) 797-6272
cole_emerson@msn.com

Points to Monitor for Changes

Asian Disaster Management News
PO box 4 Klong Luang, Pathumthani 12120 Thailand
66 02 524 5354
www.adpc.ait.ac.th

Australia—Journal of Business Continuity
2 Railway Parade, Melbourne Australia 3163
61 3 9565 1629
info@continuity.com.au

Business Continuity Magazine
The Courtyard
55 Charterhouse Street
London EC1M 6HA
44 207 608 8403
www.kablenet.com/bc

Contingency Planning & Management
84 Park Ave. Flemington NJ 08822 USA
(908) 788-0343
www.witterpublishing.com

Continuity Planner
www.continuityplanner.com
(sign up for the e-zine)

Disaster Recovery Journal
PO Box 510110 St. Louis MO 63151
(314) 894-0276
drj@drj.com

EIIP Virtual Forum
www.emforum.org/welcome.htm

Emergency Management Australia
PO Box 1020, Dickson, Australian Capital Territory 2602,
Australia
61 2 6266 5402
ema@ema.gov.au

Global Continuity
www.globalcontinuity.com

Japan Crisis Management and Preparedness Organization
03 3215 9825
rhoden@cmpo.org

Natural Hazards Observer
University of Colorado 482 UCB
Boulder CO 80309-0482
(303) 492-6818
hazctr@colorado.edu

Singapore — Calamity Prevention
76A Duxton Road Singapore 089535 65 6324 3091
www.calamityprevention.com.sg

■ BIBLIOGRAPHY FOR RESEARCH

Strategic Thinking

Schwartz, Peter. *The Art of the Long View: Planning for the Future in a Uncertain World.* New York: Doubleday, 1996

Practical Risk Analysis Surveying

Broder, James F. *Risk Analysis and the Security Survey* (2nd ed.). Boston: Butterworth-Heinemann, 1999. Available at www.bhusa.com.

Governmental Local Emergency Managers' Approach

Drabek, Thomas E., ed. *Emergency Management: Principles and Practice for Local Government.* Washington, DC: International City Management Association, 1991.

Crisis Management

Mitroff, Ian I., and Gus Anagnos. *Managing Crises before They Happen.* New York: American Management Association, 2001.

■ EMERGENCY MANAGEMENT HIGHER EDUCATION PROGRAMS IN THE UNITED STATES

There are also a number of university-based sources categorized into those offering occasional courses, undergraduate degrees, postgraduate degrees, and certificates. Most provide opportunities for high-quality continuing professional education. Some that I know are in that group are included in the following list, compiled by B. Wayne Blanchard.

Anna Maria College—master's
Arizona State University–East—bachelor's
Arizona State University–East—master's
Arkansas Tech University—bachelor's
Benedictine University, IL—MPH Disaster Management
    Concentration (2002)
Benedictine University, IL—Disaster Management
    Certificate
Caldwell Community College, NC—associate's
California State University, Long Beach—master's
California State University–Fullerton—certificate
Central Missouri State University
Clackamas Community College—associate's
Delaware Technical and Community College—associate's
Del Mar College, Corpus Christi—certificate
Eastern Michigan University—undergraduate minor
Eastern Michigan University—master's concentration
Florida International University—certificate
Florida State University—bachelor's
Florida State University—certificate
Florida State University—master's
Frontier Community College—certificate
George Washington University—certificate

George Washington University—doctoral concentration
George Washington University—master's concentration
Georgia State University—graduate certificate in emergency management
Georgia State University—MPA emergency management concentration
Georgia State University (jointly with Georgia Tech)—doctoral specialization
Jacksonville State University—master's
John Jay College, City University of NY—emergency management concentration, MA in protection management
Louisiana State University—minor in Disaster Science and Management
MCP Hahnemann University—related
Millersville University—minor
National College of Business and Technology, Puerto Rico—associate's
North Dakota State University—multidisciplinary minor in emergency management
Oklahoma State University, Environmental Management Institute—doctoral
Oklahoma State University, Department of Political Science—master's
Red Rocks Community College—associate degree in emergency management and planning
Red Rocks Community College—certificate in emergency management
Rivier College—bachelor's
Rochester Institute of Technology—certificate
Santa Monica College—partial and full certificate
Shenandoah University—certificate
St. Petersburg College—associate degree
St. Petersburg College—certificate

Texas A&M University—doctoral concentration
Texas A&M University—master's concentration
Thomas Edison State College—associate's
Thomas Edison State College—bachelor's
University of Akron—bachelor's
University of California Extension at Santa Cruz—certificate
University of Delaware—doctoral degree in environmental and energy policy with a concentration in disaster and public policy
University of Delaware—doctoral degree in sociology with a specialization in disaster studies
University of Delaware—master's degree in environmental and energy policy with a concentration in disaster and public policy
University of Delaware—master's degree in sociology with a specialization in disaster studies
University of Florida—bachelor's
University of Florida—three executive certificates
University of Florida—master's
University of Hawaii—certificate
University of North Texas—bachelor's
University of North Texas—EAMP concentration within MPA
University of North Texas—distance learning certificate
University of Richmond—undergraduate certificate
University of Richmond—associate's
University of Richmond—bachelor's
University of Richmond—graduate certificate in disaster science
University of Tennessee–Chattanooga—bachelor-level concentration
University of Tennessee–Knoxville—master's concentration

University of Utah—six emergency management certificates
University of Washington—masters emphasis area
University of Wisconsin—diploma
Western Washington University—certificate in emergency management
Woodring College of Education, WA—emergency management, emphasis in BA in human services
York County Technical College—associate's

Notes

► **Notes to Chapter 1**

1. Disaster defined.
2. One-term mayor Art Agnos was replaced by Frank Jordan in 1992.
3. *The Olympian* newspaper and Associated Press, November 8, 2001.
4. Correspondence between David Olson and the author, January 2002.
5. To Purina.
6. First Brands bought the home and products business.
7. Rhone Poulenc got the agriculture products.
8. Chronology of the Union Carbide Corporation, compiled by George Draffan, published at Endgame, www.endgame.org, accessed January 13, 2002.
9. Aviators refer to a situation deteriorating rapidly into unrecoverable flight as a graveyard spiral. That is a good match for the progression of disruptive events into disasters and on to catastrophes.
10. A list of threats (government preparedness managers say "hazards") to help planners is in Appendix A of Chapter 2.
11. Rates quotation section for *The National Enquirer* on nationwideadvertising.com, Nationwide Advertising's Web site, January 2002.
12. Conversation with Eric Norman.
13. Ian I. Mitroff and Ralph H. Kilmann, in *Corporate Tragedies* (New York: Praeger, 1984).

14. In Fink's *Crisis Management* (New York: American Management Association, 1986).
15. Tylenol's percentage of the analgesic market is from *Corporate Tragedies,* cited earlier.
16. Tylenol's remarkable recovery percentage is from *Crisis Management,* cited earlier.
17. The Tylenol case was prominent in handouts during my course in strategic planning at the University of California's Continuing Education in Business and Management.
18. Also called mobile phones or hand phones in other parts of the world.
19. For a more thorough discussion, see *Nokia vs. Ericsson: Crisis Management in the Mobile Telephone Market,* by Larry Cristini in the ContinuityPlanner.com e-zine, February, 2002.

➤ Notes to Chapter 2

1. The Business Continuity Institute is at Post Office Box 4474 Worcester WR6 5YA in the United Kingdom and can be reached at 44-870 603 8783 or by e-mail at www.thebci.org.
2. The Disaster Recovery Institute International is at 111 Park Place, Falls Church VA 22046-4513 and can be reached at (703) 538-1792; by fax at (703) 241-5603; or by e-mail at www.drii.org.
3. The International Association of Emergency Managers is at 111 Park Place, Falls Church VA 22046-4513 and can be reached at (703) 538-1795, by fax at (703) 241-5603, or by e-mail at info@iaem.com.
4. Part 29, Code of Federal Regulations, Section 1910.38 in its entirety.
5. *NFPA 1600 Standard on Disaster/Emergency Management and Business Continuity Programs* (Quincy, MA: National Fire Protection Association).
6. Various professional organizations adopt various lexicons.

Readers may try to differentiate between my *risk assessment* and the Business Continuity Institute's *risk evaluation* or between *impact estimating* and *business impact analysis*. Don't bother. At this point, such hairsplitting loses the point. Such distinctions are minutiae best left to academic discussions.

7. Chapter 4 is written to give bosses a handle on managing the project's manager.

8. Natural Hazards Center, University of Colorado at Boulder, 482UCB Boulder CO 80309-0482. Phone: (303) 492-6818. Fax: (303) 492-2151. E-mail: hazctr@colorado.edu.

9. In much of the literature of the earth scientists, *frequency* becomes *return rate*.

10. Senior managers please note: When proposed strategies are presented by planners, look for instances where the capability for more than one strategy will be required.

11. The term *critical business function* is thus defined by whether it is critical to the organization's mission. Again I must emphasize that this is the real mission.

12. I began with field team training for emergency responders in the San Francisco Bay region in 1976 and then was a classroom and simulation lab instructor for California's Specialized Training Institute until 1982.

13. Variants of this truth have been attributed to various thinkers in recent times. To my knowledge, both Barrett Tillman (in his novel *The Sixth Battle*) and Hans Ulrich Rudel ("you will only accomplish what you have practiced") have been quoted.

14. The second organizational model depicted is the multi-hazard functional planning system, as described to the author by Loren Page, at the time (early 1980s) with the California Office of Emergency Services.

15. Here again, the terminology is less important than the concept. If the reader's company uses another term for

grouping business functions with similar characteristics—called a *department* in this book—readers should substitute that term.

16. I am indebted for the concepts briefly outlined here to the lectures of Grady Bray and Jeff Mitchell, both Critical Incident Stress Debriefers and instructors at EMI. Readers who would learn more can reach them through the International Critical Incident Stress Foundation in Ellicott City, Maryland.

17. Workplace violence and a terrorist attack at first are usually indistinguishable from each other. The reader should keep this in mind when planning and training for either threat.

18. Time estimates are based on actual ERT training in my own experience. Readers should work out their own with the trainers they will use.

► Notes to Chapter 3

1. N. Dale Dunham, Emergency Planning Coordinator, San Francisco International Airport, California, January–March, 2002.

2. Richard C. Wilson, City Manager, Santa Cruz, California, 1990–1992.

3. Some names include Corporate Command Center, Corporate Crisis Center, Crisis Center, and, colloquially, the War Room.

4. First Interstate Bank's *First Interstate Fire Video*. Los Angeles, California: First Interstate Bank, May 1988. 18:44 minutes.

5. *Production,* depending on the site's functions, may be customer service, warehousing and shipping, development, and so on.

6. In recent months, I have been present during attempts to operate virtual Crisis Management Centers using telecommunications, computerized inputs and displays, and in-

formation systems linking technology. Their principal utility at this point is to link absent Crisis Management Team members to those in the Crisis Management Center.

7. I was first shown this method by Carolyn Hay-McMullen of the McMullen Co. and Loren Page of the California Governor's Office of Emergency Services as part of the multihazard functional planning system more than 25 years ago. The grid-plus-P-and-S technique has been adopted by numerous other organizations and continues to work well.

8. John Laye and Isabel Martinez Torre-Enciso, *Business Continuity as a Business Strategy* (Delft, The Netherlands: International Emergency Management Society, 1999).

9. Do I author recommend ignoring the noncritical functions? In general, yes. More on this later.

10. In California, the Governor's Office of Emergency Services has a training campus, the California Specialized Training Institute, at San Luis Obispo. Some of its courses have content close to the needs of private sector, especially Emergency Management Team members. Contact: PO Box 8123, San Luis Obispo CA 93403-8123; (805) 549-3535; CSTIinfo@oes.ca.gov.

11. EMI is about an hour's drive from Washington, D.C., in Emmitsburg, Maryland. Office of Admissions, Building I, 16825 S. Seton Avenue, Emmitsburg MD 21727; (301) 447-1035; fax, (301) 447-1441; www.fema.gov/emi.

12. The practice of describing emergency management in four phases (preparation, response, recovery, and mitigation) is a necessary convention but can mislead people without much experience into believing that there are separate and distinct activities bounded by each phase, with an exact time and criteria for switching from one to the next. Although I addressed that misconception in Chapter 2, it is worth repeating here that it just is not so.

13. The author gratefully acknowledges his debt for the concepts in the section on *Public Relations and Similar Communications* to several professional experts in this field over years of informal conversations and attending their presentations. They are Evelyn R. Young, author, reporter, mentor, and parent; Art Botterell, consultant expert in both the art and science of emergency public information; David Fowler, journalist, TV anchor, and unforgettable instructor; and David Schoumacher, combat journalist, network commentator, media entrepreneur, and insightful instructor.

14. At EMI, Emmitsburg, Maryland, from 1982 to the time of writing this in March of 2002. Also at the University of California at Berkeley's Extension courses in Continuity Education in Business and Management—Emergency Preparedness.

15. All these forms are available and downloadable from www.fs.fed.us/fire/planning/nist/ics_forms.htm.

► Notes to Chapter 4

1. Policy-level groups attending management courses, especially at EMI, write policy statements that are implemented in training exercises within days. I have mentored those groups for several years and offer this policy statement as a synthesis of the best, with the addition of what I feel would have benefited implementers most.

2. Sidebar from "Keeping a critical eye on the situation" in *Business Continuity,* Winter 2001–2002.

3. First Interstate Bank's *First Interstate Fire Video.* Los Angeles, California: First Interstate Bank, May 1988. 18:44 minutes.

4. John E. Laye and Martinez Torre-Enciso, *The Effects of Senior Management Decisions on Emergency Preparedness.* Presentation at the International Emergency Management Society's annual meeting. Toronto, Ontario, Canada, June 2002.

5. What's dangerous? Not knowing the reader's organization and its environment, I cannot give a direct answer. I can, however, provide an appendix with food for thought before the reader is put to the test. Please see Appendix A of this Chapter.

6. Professor of Economics, La Escorial University, Madrid, Spain.

➤ Notes to Chapter 5

1. Art Botterell, media Producer, consultant, and mentor. E-mail advice in September 2001 to the author after reviewing an article titled *Communicating in a Crisis,* later published by Business Partners for Emergency Preparedness, Milpitas, California.

2. Two examples are www.redcross.org/pubs/dspubs/cdelist and www.fema.gov/dizprepare.

3. These recommendations were underlined by a series of articles: "A Response to This Crisis Couldn't Be Learned in an M. B. A. Class" by Leslie Wayne and Leslie Kaufman, *New York Times,* September 16, 2001; "Disaster Planning is Serious Business" by Shu Shin Luh, *Wall Street Journal,* September 21, 2001; and "Disaster Recovery's Core Component: People" by Debra Donston, *eWEEK,* September 13, 2001.

4. Steven Fink's *Crisis Management: Planning for the Inevitable* (New York: AMACOM, 1986).

5. "Impact of 11 September on the Insurance Industry," Intellibridge report e-mailed March 11, 2001.

6. Read: Give the information to senior management before your phone goes into meltdown.

7. "Crisis Management" by Bill Patterson, in *Public Relations Journal,* November 1993.

8. I gratefully acknowledge the contributions of several professionals who shared their thoughts and advice in ad-

dressing the topics of media and internal communications: Evelyn R. Young, David Fowler, Art Botterell, Steven Fink, Mike Davies, and David Schoumacher.

➤ Notes to Chapter 6

1. Munich RE Group, "Natural Catastrophes: The Current Position," *Münchener Rückversicherungs-Gesellschaft,* Topics, Munich, December 2000.
2. Canter, M. S., and Cole, J. B. "The Foundation and Evolution of the Catastrophe Bond Market," *Global Reinsurance,* Hedge Financial Products, Inc., September 1997.
3. Laye, J. E., and Martinez Torre-Enciso, I. "Financing Catastrophe Risk in the Capital Markets," *International Journal of Emergency Management,* Vol. 1, No. 1, 2001.
4. *Intellibridge* e-mail report, March 11, 2002.
5. "Business Continuity Study" Benchmark Report. 2001. *Contingency Planning and Management* and KPMG, and *Crisis Management Survey of Fortune 1000 Companies,* 1997, The George Washington University Institute for Crisis and Disaster Management.
6. Among the good things about the digital revolution is that initial activation may be done using office desktops or home laptops *if* a virtual Crisis Management Center has been developed for this early stage. I do not recommend virtual Crisis Management Centers, except for early stages of activation and later, during deactivation. Transitions between the virtual and the physical are tricky. Practice is required.
7. "Are You Ready to Meet a Disaster?" by Virgil M. Dissmeyer in *Harvard Business Review,* May–June, 1983, Vol. 61, No. 3.

➤ Notes to Chapter 7

1. *The Terrorist Attacks on September 11, 2001: Immediate Impacts and Their Ramifications for Federal Emergency Man-*

agement by Claire B. Rubin. Quick Report No. 140, Natural Hazards Center, University of Colorado, Boulder, Colorado.

2. Discussions with Lawrence G. Olson, City Manager of Carson, California, in 1995–1997.
3. "Recovery from Disaster" by Claire B. Rubin in *Emergency Management: Principles and Practice.* Washington, DC: International City Management Association, 1991.
4. "Tribute to Rick Rescorla" by Michelle Malkin in *The Washington Times* of March 2, 2002. The same and other complimentary information is in numerous other sources.
5. Various figures are quoted among professionals, but the range is that about 35% to 50% of businesses impacted by disasters do not survive. In recent cases the corporate names have continued, but the leadership departed and the companies were considerably downsized.
6. "Has the World of Business Continuity Changed?" by David Smith in *Continuity,* Vol. 5, No. 4 (Winter 2001).
7. Discussions with City Manager Richard Wilson of Santa Cruz, California, following the Loma Prieta earthquake there, 1989–1992. Also discussions with senior managers whose organizations had experienced major disasters during courses at EMI, 1982–2002.
8. "Morgan Stanley Selling Nearly Completed Office Tower to Lehman" by Charles V. Bagli in *The New York Times* on October 9, 2001.
9. Claire B. Rubin, op. cit.
10. *Natural Hazards Observer,* Vol. 25, No. 4 (March 2001).

➤ **Notes to Chapter 8**

1. Informal interviews with Emergency Services Director Cecil L. Williams, City of Milpitas, California Fire and Rescue Services, 1995–2000.
2. There are also 37 certificate programs and 59 universities

that offer one or more courses. Information in text is from the Natural Hazards Center's Web site, Higher Education Project (2000 data).

➤ Notes to Chapter 9

1. The right board-up contractor can cover windows and vents and cable down temporary structures before forecast high winds can do extensive damage—*if* contracted before need.
2. Employers with fewer than 10 employees may communicate the plan orally and need not maintain a written plan.
3. Requires an alarm system in compliance with section 1910.165 and states that a distinctive signal shall be used if it is also to alert the fire brigade or for other purposes.
4. At this point the absence of a requirement for a written plan with fewer than 10 employees is introduced.

➤ Note to Chapter 10

1. Department of the Treasury, Office of the Controller of the Currency Circular OCC97-23.

Index